Inside Meaning
Proficiency reading comprehension

Michael Swan

Cambridge University Press
Cambridge
London · New York · Melbourne

Published by the Syndics of the Cambridge University Press
The Pitt Building, Trumpington Street, Cambridge CB2 1RP
Bentley House, 200 Euston Road, London NW1 2DB
32 East 57th Street, New York, NY 10022, USA
296 Beaconsfield Parade, Middle Park, Melbourne 3206, Australia

First published 1975
Reprinted 1977, 1978, 1979

Series design by Ken Garland and Associates

Printed in Great Britain at the
University Press, Cambridge

ISBN 0 521 20972 2 Student's Book
ISBN 0 521 22132 3 Teacher's Book
ISBN 0 521 22067 X Cassette 1
ISBN 0 521 22298 2 Cassette 2

Contents

Preface

This is a new kind of comprehension course. Its purpose is not simply to provide practice material, but to *teach*, progressively and systematically, the various skills which are necessary for successful reading comprehension. The book contains:

Nine teaching units. These provide lesson material (explanations and short exercises) on various aspects of comprehension work, such as basic reading technique, summary-writing, and the appreciation of a writer's use of language.

Twenty-six practice units. These contain texts and comprehension questions designed to give systematic practice on the points dealt with in the teaching units.

Twelve practice tests. These are similar in style to the comprehension tests in the Cambridge Proficiency examination; they can be used for pre-examination practice, for assessing students' progress, or for general revision.

The course is designed for advanced students of English as a foreign language. This book assumes a starting level about midway between the Cambridge First Certificate and the Cambridge Certificate of Proficiency. It includes a complete preparation for the various comprehension tests contained in the Proficiency examination, and can be used in the last year of a two-year Proficiency course, or in the last 3–6 months of an intensive course. However, it is not by any means intended only for examination work, but is designed for use as part of any advanced English course.

The texts cover a wide range of different types of modern English writing, and have been specially selected for the interest and variety of their subject matter and style. Most of them can be used not only for comprehension work, but also as a basis for other language-teaching activities such as class discussion or intensive vocabulary work.

A detailed description of the purpose and structure of the book, together with suggestions for its use, is given in 'Notes for teachers'. These notes are extended in the accompanying teacher's book which gives information about the authors, contexts or cultural background of the texts where this seems desirable; it also provides answers to all the questions set on the texts and suggestions for follow-up work such as writing and discussion.

Those texts which lend themselves to oral exploitation have been recorded on cassette. The teacher's book suggests ways to use the recording, for example, for global or detailed listening comprehension, pronunciation work or as an aid to oral presentation of a text intended for intensive language study.

M. S.

Acknowledgements

The author and publisher are grateful to the following for permission to reproduce quoted passages:

p. 7, Hodder and Stoughton, reprinted by permission of A. D. Peters & Co. Ltd; p. 9 from *The Raymond Chandler Omnibus*. Copyright © 1953 Raymond Chandler, Hamish Hamilton; p. 10, Jonathan Cape Ltd; p. 12, Penguin, by permission of Curtis Brown Ltd; p. 15, Collins, Sons & Co., Ltd; p. 16, Routledge & Kegan Paul Ltd; p. 18, Guardian Newspapers Ltd, 14 January 1975; p. 22, from *Images of Deviance*, ed. Stanley Cohen, Penguin, and Hulton Press (now Studio Vista Ltd) from Charles Raven, *The Underworld Nights*; p. 23, *The Observer*, 23 August 1970; p. 25, Jonathan Cape Ltd and Glidrose Productions; p. 28, Michael Joseph Ltd, © Mr Richard Condon; p. 30, reproduced from *The Times* by permission, 28 November 1974; p. 31, Methuen & Co. Ltd; p. 37, Guardian Newspapers Ltd, 29 November 1971; p. 41, reproduced by permission of *Punch*; p. 43, from *New Horizons in Psychology*, ed. Brian Foss, Penguin, 1966; p. 47, Mr Christopher Johnson, p. 48, reproduced from *The Times* by permission, 12 March 1975; p. 56, from *Images of Deviance*, ed. S. Cohen, © Penguin Books Ltd 1971; R. Blum quoted from *Utopiates*, Tavistock Publications Ltd; Detective Inspector Wyatt quoted from *The Times Educational Supplement*, by permission; p. 57, from *Linguistics at Large*, ed. Noel Minnis, Victor Gollancz Ltd; p. 59, Jonathan Cape Ltd; p. 61, Routledge & Kegan Paul Ltd; p. 63, Harper & Row, New York; p. 64, Krishnamurti Foundation Trust and Victor Gollancz Ltd; p. 65, from *Oddly Enough*, Max Reinhardt Ltd; p. 66 reprinted by permission of Petersen Publishing Co. from *Guns and Ammo* Magazine, December 1974; p. 67, Baltimore, Md.: Penguin Books Inc, 1972. Copyright © Alternatives Foundation 1971; p. 69, Chatto & Windus Ltd; p. 70, Longman Group Ltd; p. 71, Mrs Sonia Brownell Orwell and Secker & Warburg; p. 72, Guardian Newspapers Ltd, 9 October 1974; p. 74, Allen Lane 1971/Penguin 1972. Copyright © Charles A. Reich 1970; p. 76, this article first appeared on 2 May 1974 in *New Scientist*, London. The weekly review of Science and Technology; p. 78, *The Observer*, 22 September 1974; p. 80, reproduced from *The Times* by permission, 29 November 1974; p. 82, from *War and Democracy*, Routledge & Kegan Paul Ltd; pp. 87 and 90, Collins Fontana and *The Observer*; p. 92, Jonathan Cape Ltd; p. 93, Society of Authors; p. 95, from *Lord Arthur Savile's Crime and Other Stories*, Penguin; p. 96, William Heinemann Ltd; p. 97, the Executors of the Ernest Hemingway Estate and Jonathan Cape Ltd; p. 97, from *Quite Early one Morning*, J. M. Dent & Sons Ltd and the Trustees for the Copyrights of the late Dylan Thomas; p. 98, Guardian Newspapers Ltd, 1 November 1974; p. 100, Department of Education and Science, and Her Majesty's Stationery Office; p. 100, Rupert Chetwynd & Partners Ltd, for Royal Viking Line; p. 101, Department of Energy, by permission of the Controller of Her Majesty's Stationery Office, Crown copyright; p. 105, Michael Joseph Ltd; p. 106, Max Reinhardt Ltd; p. 108, Chapman & Hall, reprinted by permission of A. D. Peters & Co. Ltd; p. 109, reprinted from *Chicago Seed*, vol. 8, no. 9; p. 111, *Spare Rib*, August 1973; p. 113, Guardian Newspapers Ltd, 15 October 1974; p. 115, from *New Horizons in*

Psychology, ed. Brian Foss. © Penguin Books Ltd 1966; p. 118, Granada Publishing Ltd; p. 120, Guardian Newspapers Ltd, 18 November 1974; p. 122, reprinted with permission of Reuters, 18 May 1970; p. 124, *The Observer*, 8 March 1975; p. 127, Guardian Newspapers Ltd, 2 December 1974; p. 129, Pelican, © Mr H. J. Eysenck; p. 130 © 1975 by the New York Times Company. Reprinted by permission; p. 131, reproduced from *The Times* by permission, 14 March 1975; p. 132, Routledge & Kegan Paul Ltd; p. 134, Michael Joseph Ltd, © Mr Richard Condon.

Notes for teachers

What exactly is 'reading comprehension'?

If we say that a student is 'good at comprehension', we mean that he can read accurately and efficiently, so as to get the maximum information from a text with the minimum of misunderstanding. We may also mean (though this is not quite the same) that he is able to show his understanding by re-expressing the content of the text – for instance, by writing sentences or paragraphs in answer to questions, or by summarising the text.

Language is not the only factor in successful comprehension: some students who speak and write English very well are poor at this kind of work, and of course people may be bad at comprehension even in their own mother tongue.

Some of the reasons for failure in comprehension are connected with defective reading habits. Not all students read efficiently, even in their own language, and there are several things that can go wrong:

a) Some students find it difficult to 'see the wood for the trees'. They may read slowly and carefully, paying a lot of attention to individual points, but without succeeding in getting a clear idea of the overall meaning of a text.

b) Other students (especially those who read quickly) do not always pay enough attention to detail. They may have a good idea of the general meaning of the text, but misunderstand particular points. Sometimes, by overlooking an important small word (for instance a conjunction, a negation, a modal verb) they may get a completely false impression of the meaning of part of the passage.

c) Some students are 'imaginative readers': especially if they know something about the subject, or have strong opinions about it, they may interpret the text in the light of their own experience and viewpoints, so that they find it difficult to separate what the writer says from what they feel themselves.

Other types of comprehension problem arise directly from the text. Even when a student is familiar with all the words and structures in a passage, complexities in the way the writer expresses himself may present obstacles to efficient comprehension.

d) Long and complicated sentences are difficult to cope with in a foreign language; even when the words are easy, syntactic complexity may cause a reader to lose the thread.

e) Some writers favour a wordy and repetitive style; practice is needed to be able to 'see through' the words to the (often very simple) ideas which underlie them.

f) A writer may express an important idea indirectly. In order to understand some texts, one needs to be sensitive to the implications of a remark: to draw the necessary inferences from what is not stated directly. This is of course particularly difficult in a foreign language.

g) Words and expressions which the student does not know obviously present a problem (unless he is working with a dictionary). However, students do not always realise how easy it is to guess many unknown words simply by studying the context. Some students, indeed, are so disturbed by unfamiliar vocabulary that their comprehension of the whole passage suffers.

Finally, some 'comprehension' examinations test skills which go beyond the limits of comprehension proper. (For instance, the ability to summarise, or to comment on a writer's use of language.) Most students, even those who are good at reading and understanding, need additional training to be able to cope with tests of this kind.

In this book, the various problems referred to above are separated out, and specific training is provided in each of the skills involved. The teaching units contain explanations and exercises designed to help students to read accurately (seeing both the overall plan and the details of a text), to guess unknown words, to draw inferences, and to deal with complex sentences and 'wordy' writing. Special sections of the book cover 'open-ended' comprehension questions, including summary, and 'perception of the effective use of English'.

Structure of the book

The book contains four main sections (for a detailed plan see the list of contents). These are:

Section A   Basic reading technique and multiple choice tests
Section B   Open-ended tests and summary-writing
Section C   Perception of the effective use of English
Section D   Practice tests

Each of the first three sections contains two or more teaching units. A teaching unit is designed for classwork, and contains introductory explanations and exercises on a specific element of comprehension technique (e.g. accurate reading, writing summaries, appreciation of a writer's use of language).

Each teaching unit is followed by a number of practice units (suitable for classwork or homework), containing texts and questions. The practice units give further work on the point dealt with in the teaching unit, together with general comprehension practice and revision of points dealt with earlier.

The fourth section contains twelve practice tests, similar in form to the comprehension tests in the Cambridge Proficiency examination; these can be used as a 'run-up' for candidates in the last weeks before the examination, or for other purposes (such as assessing students' progress).

How to use the book

Obviously the exercises and materials in this book can be used in various ways, and experienced teachers will adopt whatever approach is best suited to their style of teaching and the needs of their classes. The following notes are intended merely as suggestions.

a) Since the book is progressive (both the texts and the exercises are graded roughly in order of difficulty), it is on the whole advisable to work through the teaching units 'from left to right' – that is, in the order in which they come in the book. Section A, in particular, provides a basic training in reading technique (as well as practice in multiple choice tests), and if students spend plenty of time on this part they will find it easier to cope with the more advanced problems that arise in sections B and C.

b) After doing a teaching unit, there is no need to do all the practice units which follow. One at least should be done straight away (either for homework or in the next comprehension lesson); if time allows and more practice is needed on the point involved, teachers may wish to do two practice units before going on to the next teaching unit.

Other practice units can be dropped, or used for revision at a later stage (the last practice unit in each group is often more difficult than the others, and therefore more suitable for revision work). Note that in the section on writing summaries there are more practice units than usual in order to give adequate work on this point, which some students find especially difficult.

c) Handling a teaching unit in class. As well as introductory exercises on the point being taught, the teaching units contain explanations addressed directly to the students. These are not, of course, intended to replace the teacher's lesson on the point: their purpose is to provide students with a simple guide which they can refer to when preparing or revising the work done in class. Teachers will decide for themselves how to present and work through the teaching unit material; three possible approaches are as follows:

(i) Begin by giving your own lesson on the relevant point (modifying or supplementing the teaching apparatus in the book to suit your own approach and the needs of your class). Then work through the exercise material with the class. This can be done orally, or students can write their answers and then discuss them. Group work can be very effective with some of the exercises: students can work together to produce answers to the questions, or they can write their answers individually and then join together into groups to compare and discuss what they have written.

(ii) Ask the students to prepare the lesson by reading the teaching unit at home before the class. Class time can then be devoted to doing the exercises and discussing the problems which arise.

(iii) If class time is short, simply give a brief lesson on the point dealt with in the unit, and ask the students to read the unit and do the exercises for homework.

Note that the teaching units vary in length; with some of the longer ones, it may be necessary to spend two classes on the unit, or to begin the unit in class and ask the students to finish it for homework.

Some of the teaching units cover, at a more advanced level, comprehension topics which have been dealt with in *Understanding Ideas*. Students who have successfully worked through *Understanding Ideas* may not need to cover the same ground again in class, and can go straight on to the practice units.

d) On the whole, it is advisable for students to do their comprehension classwork and homework without dictionaries. Dictionaries are not allowed in most language examinations, and it is, in any case, important for advanced students to get used to dealing confidently with unfamiliar vocabulary (see teaching unit 2, 'Guessing unknown words'). Where a text contains a difficult word or expression which could prevent comprehension of the whole passage, the meaning is explained in a footnote.

e) For examination candidates, timing is important and there is often a good deal of work to be done in a short time. As the examination approaches, it is a good idea to give time limits for the practice units, reducing these progressively until students are able to work efficiently at speed. Shortly before the examination, it is very valuable for students to do some practice examination papers under strict examination conditions: the practice tests at the end of the book can be used to provide the comprehension sections of these.

Beyond comprehension

The exercises in the book are designed particularly to give students training in reading comprehension. However, many of the texts deserve more than this. It would be a pity, for instance, to study the description of bewildered working-class children starting grammar school (page 132) without asking students if they have had similar experiences. Again, if one has read Abbie Hoffman's amusing instructions for undermining the capitalist system (page 109), one will obviously want to ask students for their reactions. Once a passage has been understood, it can be used (among other things) for intensive vocabulary work, semi-controlled composition, and in many cases discussion. The following suggestions may be helpful.

Intensive vocabulary work. The best approach here is probably to select for teaching a limited number (perhaps 10–20) of words and expressions from the text. These should obviously be items which the students cannot yet use correctly (though they may already understand them), but they should be common and preferably useful for speech as well as writing. If the students are going to do writing or discussion work related to the text, the words and expressions ought to be chosen with this in mind. When these words and expressions have been explained and practised, give the students time to study them and then (perhaps in the next lesson), give a 'recall test' – that is to say, ask questions to which the answers are the items that were studied.

Semi-controlled composition. Vocabulary is not usually learnt very effectively unless it is actually used to express something. A good approach is to follow up intensive vocabulary work with a composition exercise. In this, students are asked to write about a subject similar to that of the text, so that they can use the new words and expressions to convey their own ideas. (For example, after studying *Traveller's tales*, p. 90, students could write an imaginary dialogue between a native of their own country and an Englishman who has never been there but thinks he knows all about it.) Make sure that students understand that they are expected to use words and expressions from the text, and that they realise why this is important.

Discussion. Some of the texts can be used as a basis for discussion. This is probably most effective after vocabulary study and writing work have been done, so that students are familiar with some of the words and expressions they will need.

Grouping texts. In order to facilitate discussion and composition work, two or three texts on similar subjects can be studied in combination. Texts which could be grouped in this way are:

   Grammar school (p. 132), *Adolescent students* (p. 63) and *Education: a father's experience* (p. 61)
   The bohemian marihuana smoker (p. 56) and *Legalising pot* (p. 127)
   Teaching speech (p. 69), *Received pronunciation* (p. 70) and *Washoe* (p. 57)
   Violence (p. 64), *The causes of conflict* (p. 81) and *Gun control* (p. 66)
   Bat Dongin (p. 28), *A car chase* (p. 25) and *Gunfight in Pickering City* (p. 134)

Note: contracted forms

Students are sometimes told that contractions such as *don't, it's, they'll* are only used in writing down direct speech. This is not, of course, true: contractions are common in informal written English of all kinds, and they will be found in many of the texts in this book. The instructions to students in the teaching units are deliberately written in a casual, informal style, and these too contain contractions. However, students who use the book should perhaps be warned not to use contractions themselves when a more formal style is appropriate: they should realise clearly that contractions would be out of place, for instance, in a job application or a serious essay in an examination.

Section A:
Basic reading technique and multiple choice tests

Teaching unit 1: How to read a text

In this unit you are going to practise the technique of reading a text so as to understand the meaning as clearly as possible. It is generally a good idea to read a comprehension passage at least twice: once to get an overall impression of what it is about, and then a second time to concentrate on the details. Read much more slowly than you would read a novel or a newspaper article – most people read comprehension texts far too fast. Time spent reading is saved later, because you can answer the questions more quickly and accurately.

First reading

Read this text once, not too fast, and then do the exercise which follows.

Graduates

The new prestige of the British graduate is the more spectacular because in the past Britain has been much less interested in universities and degrees than other advanced countries – or even some backward ones. In 1901 Ramsay Muir observed that Britain had fewer universities per head than any other civilized country in Europe except Turkey. A UNESCO survey in 1967 showed Britain still close to the bottom in Europe, in terms of the proportion of the age-group from twenty to twenty-four who were enrolled in higher education. Most continental countries in the last decade have expanded their higher education faster than Britain. University statistics are notoriously difficult to compare, because of the different implications of the word 'student'; in most continental countries anyone who passes his final school exam – the *baccalauréat* or *abitur* – is entitled to go into the university on the principle of 'laissez-passer'*; but he has no guarantees of tuition or personal attention. Partly as a result there are far more drop-outs and 'ghost students'; in France half the students never become graduates. A comparison of graduates, as opposed to students, shows Britain in a more favourable light, for most British students take a degree. But even in terms of graduates, Britain is still low in the Europe league.

Going to university is a much more solid ambition among the sons of the bourgeoisie in France or Germany than in Britain; many of the British middle-classes – particularly the shopkeepers and small-business men – have tended to be sceptical, if not actually hostile, to university education for their children, and there are still rich and quite intelligent parents who will prefer their children to go straight from school into the city, to the army or to farming. But the attractions of a BA or an MA have penetrated into areas, both among the rich and the poor, where they would not have been felt twenty years ago; and there are far-reaching social repercussions in the high proportion of

5
10
15
20

* *laissez-passer*: French for 'let him pass'

students who are first-generation undergraduates, who come from homes without a
university tradition. Here, too, Britain is in marked contrast to the continent: the   25
UNESCO survey of 1967 showed Britain with a much higher proportion of working-
class students (a quarter) than any other western European country.

From *The New Anatomy of Britain* by Anthony Sampson

Exercise a

Answer the following questions without looking at the text. You can answer in a word,
a short phrase, or a complete sentence, just as you like. If you have a lot of difficulty with
the exercise, it probably means that you read the text too fast.

1 In general, what is the passage about?
2 According to the passage, is there a new attitude to degrees in Britain today or not?
3 What did Ramsay Muir say in 1901? (Give the main idea; it does not matter about the
   exact words.)
4 Does Britain have more or fewer students (in proportion to her population) than most
   European countries?
5 Does Britain have more or fewer graduates (in proportion to her population) than most
   European countries?
6 Does Britain have more or fewer working-class students (in proportion to the whole
   student population) than most European countries?
7 What sort of attitude to university education has traditionally been found among the
   British middle classes?
8 Is this changing?

Second reading

Now read the text again. This time, read even more slowly, and pay special attention to
points that seem difficult. Do not read a sentence until you have understood the sentence
before as well as you can. If there is a word you do not know, do not waste too much time
worrying about what it might mean. Look at what comes before and after, make an
intelligent guess at the meaning, and then go on.
   When you think you are ready, try the next exercise.

Exercise b: Same or different?

Some of the following sentences say the same thing as part of the text; others have a different
meaning. Write the numbers of the sentences, and put S (= same) or D (= different) after
each one. You can look at the text if you want to.

Example:
a) *In 1967 UNESCO carried out a survey on higher education. Answer: 1S.*
b) *Britain has more universities than most European countries. Answer: 2D*

1 British graduates are more spectacular than they used to be.
2 In 1901 Britain had more universities, in proportion to her population, than Turkey.
3 Ramsay Muir suggested that some countries in Europe were uncivilised.
4 The UNESCO survey carried out by the Ministry of Education in 1967 showed that
   Britain had a low proportion of adults in higher education.
5 British higher education has grown relatively slowly in the last ten years.

6 The word 'student' does not mean exactly the same in all countries.

7 Many French students never graduate, but in Britain most people get a degree.

8 British middle-class attitudes to university education are mixed.

9 Wide social changes are being caused by the large number of 'first-generation' university students.

10 A quarter of British working-class students go to university.

Check your answers (you may like to discuss them with other students first). If you got several wrong, it means that you did not pay enough attention to detail: be careful to look very thoroughly at *all* the words, both in the text and in the questions.

Implication

Writers do not always express things directly – sometimes they imply them. That is to say, they suggest things in a roundabout, indirect way, so that you have to think carefully to see what they mean. It can be difficult to grasp implications in a foreign language: the following exercise will give you some useful practice. Read the text slowly twice, and then try to answer the questions.

The Hollywood Indian

The Indian smelled. He smelled clear across the little reception room when the buzzer sounded and I opened the door between to see who it was. He stood just inside the corridor door looking as if he had been cast in bronze*. He was a big man from the waist up and he had a big chest. He looked like a bum.

He wore a brown suit of which the coat was too small for his shoulders and his 5 trousers were probably a little tight under the armpits. His hat was at least two sizes too small and had been perspired in freely by somebody it fitted better than it fitted him. He wore it about where a house wears a wind vane. His collar had the snug fit of a horse-collar and was of about the same shade of dirty brown. A tie dangled outside his buttoned jacket, a black tie which had been tied with a pair of pliers in a knot the size of a pea. 10 Around his bare and magnificent throat, above the dirty collar, he wore a wide piece of black ribbon, like an old woman trying to freshen up her neck.

He had a big flat face and a high-bridged fleshy nose that looked as hard as the prow of a cruiser. He had lidless eyes, drooping jowls, the shoulders of a blacksmith and the short and apparently awkward legs of a chimpanzee. I found out later that they were only 15 short.

If he had been cleaned up a little and dressed in a white nightgown, he would have looked like a very wicked Roman senator.

His smell was the earthy smell of primitive man, and not the slimy dirt of cities.

'Huh,' he said. 'Come quick. Come now.' 20

I backed into my office and wiggled my finger at him and he followed me making as much noise as a fly makes walking on the wall. I sat down behind my desk and squeaked my swivel chair professionally and pointed to the customer's chair on the other side. He didn't sit down. His small black eyes were hostile.

'Come where?' I said. 25

He snorted and his nostrils got very wide. They had been wide enough for mouseholes to start with.

* *bronze*: a metal

'What can I do for you?'

We sneered at each other across the desk for a moment. He sneered better than I did. Then he removed his hat with massive disgust and turned it upside down. He rolled a finger around under the sweatband. That turned the sweatband up into view, and it had not been misnamed. He removed a paper clip from the edge and threw a fold of tissue paper on the desk. He pointed at it angrily, with a well-chewed fingernail. His lank hair had a shelf around it, high up, from the too-tight hat.　　　　　　　　　　　30

I unfolded the piece of tissue paper and found a card inside.　　　　　　　　　35

I played with my pipe, stared at the Indian and tried to ride him with my stare. He looked as nervous as a brick wall.

From *Farewell My Lovely* by Raymond Chandler

Exercise c

Write as simply and directly as you can what you think is meant or implied by the following expressions in the text.

Example:

'*His hat . . . had been perspired in freely by somebody it fitted better than it fitted him.*' (lines 6–7)

Answer:

It was a dirty old hat; somebody else had owned it before the Indian.

1 '. . . looking as if he had been cast in bronze' (line 3)
2 'He was a big man from the waist up' (line 3)
3 '. . . his trousers were probably a little tight under the armpits' (lines 5–6)
4 'He wore it about where a house wears a wind vane' (lines 7–8)
5 '. . . the snug fit of a horse-collar' (line 8)
6 'I found out later that they were only short' (lines 15–16)
7 '. . . making as much noise as a fly makes walking on the wall' (lines 21–2)
8 'They had been wide enough for mouseholes to start with' (lines 26–7)
9 '. . . it had not been misnamed' (lines 31–2)
10 'He looked as nervous as a brick wall' (line 37)

Practice unit 1.1

Read each text slowly and carefully (preferably twice, the first time to get a general impression and the second time to study the details). Then answer the questions that follow.

First passage

Barbara's father

At nine that evening I rolled into the club, and bumped into Barbara's father, who gave a startled cry.

'Hullo,' I said, trying not to laugh. 'I was looking for Bertie Bentall.'

He looked round helpfully. 'I don't believe I—'

'How're things, Mr Hutchinson?' I said.　　　　　　　　　　　　　　　　5

As Barbara's old man he had got me into this club rather against my will about a minute

before our engagement came to an untidy end and he found himself with Gobbo for
a son-in-law; this was the first time he'd spoken to me since, but he was the best of the
Hutchinson bunch, even now Barbara had improved as a result of marriage. It was
a severe shock for him when I first declared for Barbara and his only solace at the time   10
had been that at least she'd been spared Gobbo, so that that year had been one of the ones
he'd remember.

    'They're very well, John, very well. I hear you are doing very well for yourself.'

    'I've ground to a stop at present but I had some breaks,' I agreed. 'Oh well—'

    'We have a long-standing intention to dine together, John,' he said suddenly.   15

    'So we have,' I smiled. 'What a memory. What a sense of duty. How's your wife?'
I couldn't stand her.

    'Very well.' It turned out a little while later that he couldn't stand her himself, and they
parted, but while they were presumably drifting away from one another he was always
ready with an eager expression of good-will if anybody mentioned her. I didn't hold   20
this against him.

    He went on: 'Let's dine out rather than at home, shall we?'

    'Eat with me,' I said. 'I've a girl who cooks terribly well.'

    'Oh.'

    'Or out, I don't mind.'   25

    'Yes, let's.'

    'Excellent.'

    'I'll phone you at home. What's your number, John?'

    I told him and we parted. The best performance I ever saw Hutchinson put up was
the pleased speech he made at Barbara's wedding. In a thousand years you'd never have   30
guessed what he was thinking.

From *It Wasn't Me* by Ian Jefferies

Exercise a

For each of the following questions, you are given four possible answers.
Choose the answer that you think is best, and write the number of the question and the
letter of the correct answer. (For example, if you think the first answer to question 1 is the
best one, write 1 a.)

1 Barbara's father looked round helpfully (line 4)
a) to look at the person who had bumped into him.
b) to look for Bertie Bentall.
c) because he was startled.
d) because he did not want to look at the man who had bumped into him.

2 The narrator (the person who is telling the story) went into the club
a) because he was a member.
b) to find Barbara's father.
c) to find somebody else.
d) to invite Barbara's father to dinner.

3 He had joined the club
a) when he was engaged to Mr Hutchinson's daughter.
b) when Barbara married Gobbo.
c) against Barbara's father's will.
d) to please his fiancée.

4   Barbara's father said 'I don't believe I—' (line 4). He might have continued:
a)   remember you
b)   have seen him
c)   want to talk to you
d)   have seen you for a long time

5   Mr Hutchinson was
a)   the narrator's father-in-law.
b)   the narrator's ex-father-in-law.
c)   Gobbo's father-in-law.
d)   Barbara's father-in-law.

6   This was 'the first time he'd spoken to me since' (line 8). What do you think is the most probable reason for this?
a)   Because they had not met.
b)   Because they had avoided each other.
c)   Because they did not know each other very well.
d)   Because he had been angry.

7   Why had that year 'been one of the ones he'd remember' (lines 11–12)?
a)   Because Barbara had not married the narrator.
b)   Because she had been spared Gobbo.
c)   Because he did not like the narrator.
d)   Because Barbara had first been engaged to one unsuitable man, and then married another.

8   What is meant by 'they' in 'They're very well' (line 13)?
a)   Barbara and Gobbo
b)   things
c)   his wife and daughter
d)   the ones he'd remember

9   'I didn't hold this against him' (lines 20–1) means:
a)   I didn't argue with him about it.
b)   I didn't talk to him about it.
c)   I didn't use it to damage him.
d)   I didn't think worse of him because of it.

10 'In a thousand years you'd never have guessed what he was thinking' (lines 30–1). How do you think he felt?
a)   pleased
b)   sorry to lose his beloved daughter
c)   hostile to his wife
d)   upset that Barbara was marrying Gobbo

Second passage

The Milestone Buttress

After breakfast the proprietor introduced us to the mystery man.
    'This is Dr Richardson,' he said. 'He's very kindly agreed to take you out and teach you the rudiments of climbing.'
    'Have you ever done any?' asked the Doctor.
    It seemed no time to bring up my scrambles in the Dolomites.
    'No.' I said firmly, 'neither of us knows the first thing about it.'   5

We had arrived at seven; by nine o'clock we were back in the station wagon, this time
bound for the north face of the mountain called Tryfan.

'Stop here,' said the Doctor. Hugh parked the car by a mile-stone that read 'Bangor
X Miles'. Rearing up above the road was a formidable-looking chunk of rock, the   10
Milestone Buttress.

'That's what you're going to climb,' said the Doctor. 'It's got practically everything
you need at this stage.'

It seemed impossible. In a daze we followed him over a rough wall and into the bracken.
A flock of mountain sheep watched us go, making noises that sounded suspiciously   15
like laughter.

Finally we reached the foot of it. Close-to it didn't seem so formidable. The whole face
was scarred by the nailed boots of countless climbers.

'This thing is like a by-pass,' said the Doctor. 'Later in the season you'd have to queue
up to climb it. We're lucky to have it to ourselves.'   20

'If there's one thing we don't need it's an audience.'

'First of all you've got to learn about the rope. Without a rope climbing is suicide.
It's the only thing that justifies it.'

He showed us how to rope ourselves together, using the proper knots; how to hold
it and how to coil it so that it would pay out without snarling up, and how to belay.   25

'You never move without a proper belay. I start to climb and I go on until I reach a
knob of rock on to which I can belay. I take a *karabiner*' (he produced one of the D-shaped
steel rings with a spring-loaded clip) 'and attach a sling to the loop of rope round my waist.
Then all I have to do is to put the sling over the knob of rock, and pass the rope under
one shoulder and over the other. If possible, you brace your feet against a solid block.   30
Like that you can take the really big strain if the next man comes off.'

'What I don't see,' I whispered to Hugh, 'is what happens if the leader falls on the
first pitch. According to this he's done for.'

'The leader just mustn't fall off.'

'Remind me to let you be leader.'   35

The Doctor now showed what I thought was a misplaced trust in us. He sent us to the
top of a little cliff, not more than twenty feet high, with a battered-looking holly tree
growing on it. 'I want you to pretend that you're the leader,' he said to Hugh. 'I want
you to belay yourself with a sling and a *karabiner* to the holly tree. On the way up I am
going to fall off backwards and I shan't tell you when I'm going to do it. You've got   40
to hold me.' He began to climb.

He reached the top and was just about to step over the edge when, without warning,
he launched himself backwards into space. And then the promised miracle happened,
for the rope was taut and Hugh was holding him, not by the belay but simply with the rope
passed under one shoulder and over the other. There was no strain on the sling round   45
Hugh's waist at all, his body was like a spring. I was very impressed – for the first time
I began to understand the trust that climbers must be able to have in one another.

From *A Short Walk in the Hindu Kush* by Eric Newby

Exercise b

Choose the best answer (only one in each case).

1   The general theme of the passage is
a) learning to climb.
b) learning to fall properly.

c) the relationship which develops between Hugh, the Doctor and the narrator.

d) how to climb the Milestone Buttress.

2   What climbing experience did they have?

a) Hugh and the narrator had climbed before in the Dolomites.

b) They had learnt the rudiments of climbing, but pretended they had not.

c) They had apparently not climbed much before.

d) The narrator had climbed a good deal in the Dolomites.

3   They were going to climb the Milestone Buttress because

a) it was a good place for beginners to learn.

b) it seemed impossible.

c) there was nobody on it that day.

d) they had a rope and a good teacher.

4   At the Milestone Buttress

a) there were lots of climbers.

b) there were nails from climbers' boots.

c) there were signs that lots of climbers had been there before.

d) there was a by-pass.

5   In the expression 'it's the only thing' (line 23), 'it' refers to

a) suicide.

b) climbing.

c) the rope.

d) the whole of the previous sentence.

6   In the expression 'that justifies it' (line 23), 'it' refers to

a) suicide.

b) climbing.

c) the rope.

d) the whole of the previous sentence.

7   In line 25, 'it' refers to

a) the knot.

b) the rope.

c) the rock.

d) the belay.

8   According to the passage, 'to belay' is

a) to find a safe place to stand on a rock face.

b) to pull up the next climber.

c) to take the really big strain if the next climber comes off.

d) to fix oneself to the rock.

9   The leader must not fall off on the first pitch

a) because he is the best climber.

b) because of the trust that climbers must be able to have in one another.

c) because he is not protected by a belay.

d) because he is done for.

10 Why did the Doctor fall off?

a) Because of his misplaced trust in the others.

b) To show them something about climbing with a rope.

c) To test the belay.

d) By accident.

Practice unit 1.2

Read each text slowly and carefully (preferably twice, the first time to get a general impression and the second time to study the details). Then answer the questions that follow.

First passage

The bomb

The sweat was dangerous now and I wiped my hand on my coat before reaching up and taking the bomb from its perch on top of the exhaust-pipe. The set-up was that when I started the engine the vibration of the pipe would dislodge the bomb within the first few minutes of driving and it would hit the ground. Even at high speed the thing *must* fall immediately below the car. 5

I held it snug on my chest and slid out from under, standing up and listening from sheer habit. The night was mine.

The lock-ups were communal, with only three main partitions six feet high, and there was a side door at the far end, so I checked the gear for neutral and started the engine, moving round to the front of the car and resting the bomb on the slope of the bonnet 10 about a third of the distance from the front edge, where the smooth plastic would slide on the smooth cellulose, given time. The engine was cold and the vibration at its highest. I stood and watched the bomb in the light of the torch. In fifteen seconds it began to slide and I kept my hand ready in case. Twenty seconds and it sped up and reached my hand. 15

I wanted roughly one minute, so I put the bomb a couple of inches higher than the first time and left it there, climbing the first partition and dropping over, climbing the second and dropping, kicking over an oil-tin and disregarding the noise, climbing the third partition and making for the side door.

When I was outside I shut the door after me and sat down with my back to the garage 20 wall. I could hear the engine of the Mercedes throbbing very faintly. Sixty seconds had gone by. I went on waiting.

Ninety seconds. I had misjudged the slope of the bonnet, put the thing too high. The throb of the engine was settling, with the automatic choke easing off and the mixture thinning. The sharpness of the carbon monoxide soured the air. 25

Two minutes. It might stick there forever or it might go on creeping and finally drop. I didn't want to go and have a look. The engine was barely audible now; the temperature gauge would have moved out of the cold sector; oil pressure would be dropping a fraction.

There would be three phases. Initial percussion, audible blast and air shock-wave. Fire 30 was a certainty because of all the petrol about.

Two minutes and a half. The sweat-glands began working again. There was absolutely no way of timing a check-up safely. A whole team of picked scientists could sit here for weeks without succeeding in telling me *when* it would be safe for me to go and find out what was happening to that *bloody* thing. 35

Three minutes. If nothing happened in another ten minutes I'd have to go and take a look.

Three phases now operating. Percussion – the ground shook and the wall shuddered at my back. Audible blast – a crash of wild music as the roof went up and the glass over

the courtyard shattered and fell away in a drift to the ground. Air shock-wave – the hot 40
wind of it fanned past my face, stinking of sodium chlorate.

From *The Quiller Memorandum* by Adam Hall, adapted

Exercise a: Same or different?

Look carefully at the following statements. Then write the numbers of the statements,
followed by S if you **think** they mean the same as what is said in the text, and by D if you
think the meaning is different.

1   The narrator wiped his hand because it was wet and he was afraid of dropping the bomb.
2   Somebody had put the bomb on his exhaust-pipe in order to kill him.
3   It was very important for the bomb to fall immediately below the car at high speed.
4   He decided to explode the bomb by putting it on the car bonnet and using the vibrations
    from the engine to make it slide off.
5   He hoped that someone else would come along and get killed in the explosion.
6   He put the bomb about a third of the distance from the front of the bonnet so that
    he would have enough time to get away.
7   He was too frightened to worry about the noise from the oil-tin he kicked over.
8   He sat against the garage wall so that nobody would see him waiting for the explosion.
9   The bomb took longer than he had expected to fall off.
10 This was because he had calculated badly.

Second passage

A level chemistry

I reckon I can do A level chem. in four terms. Four terms flat out, mind. We have to go
really fast. We have tests twice a week, but we get results. For instance, last year I got an
open* at Pembroke, Cambridge, and an exhibition at Trinity Hall, Cambridge, and
then I got half-a-dozen places. I've got 14 places in the last two years and then these opens
I do pretty well; my results are all right. The way we teach, we teach for results. I want   5
the passes, the schols, and all those things. Tests all the time, and scrub the teaching
methods, forget about the educational side. Yes, it *is* like that; not altogether of course,
but there are two ways, aren't there? There's the one way I teach, and there's another
way. Well, let me give you an instance: if a boy asks a question it might raise some
interesting matters. Now, the other way you'd waste the whole period and follow up   10
those matters and that's all right. But that's not our way. We've got no time for any
questions or anything that leads off the syllabus. You've got to get through it. I like
teaching our A stream boys but you should see our C stream! They're shocking, absolutely shocking. I don't like teaching them at all, and I don't know what it can be like
in the secondary modern schools. I'm not made out for missionary teaching. What   15
I want now is a head of department in a really good school, and then I'd do what our
head of department has done. I'd put on the pressure, really hard. Really work those
children, tests, tests, tests, and get the results. Get them the results they should have,
and that would establish me, wouldn't it? It would give me a reputation. People would
know that I could do the job, I might slacken off when I got established – perhaps after   20

* *an open*: a kind of scholarship

ten years or so, I might start looking around and thinking more about the educational side. But you've got to establish yourself first, haven't you? Right?

From an interview quoted in *Education and the Working Class* by Brian Jackson and Dennis Marsden

Exercise b

Choose the best answer to each question.

1 This passage is taken from an interview with
a) a very successful chemistry student.
b) a teacher of chemistry.
c) a head of department.
d) a professor.

2 The general theme of the passage is
a) how to pass examinations.
b) how to train pupils to understand chemistry.
c) how to give tests in chemistry.
d) how to get pupils through examinations in chemistry.

3 When he says 'I've got 14 places in the last two years', the person speaking is referring to
a) offers of teaching posts.
b) offers of university places for himself.
c) offers of university places for his pupils.
d) jobs he has had.

4 He is mainly interested in
a) high-pressure teaching for examinations.
b) teaching methods.
c) the educational side.
d) answering questions which raise interesting matters.

5 What does the speaker mean by 'the other way' (line 10)?
a) an undisciplined approach to teaching
b) an approach to teaching which concentrates on passing examinations
c) answering questions which do not raise interesting matters
d) paying more attention to educational values than to examination preparation

6 If a boy asks a question
a) he follows it up if it raises an interesting point.
b) he prefers to keep to the syllabus.
c) what he does depends on whether he is teaching the A stream or the C stream.
d) he puts on the pressure.

7 'I'm not made out for missionary teaching' (line 15) means
a) I don't want to teach less intelligent pupils.
b) I don't want to teach religion.
c) I don't want to be a travelling teacher.
d) I don't want to teach things that are not on the syllabus.

8   His ambition is
a) to replace his head of department.
b) to be in charge of the chemistry teaching in a really good school.
c) to think more about the educational side.
d) to become a headmaster.

9   In the sentence 'It would give me a reputation' (line 19), 'it' refers to
a) being established.
b) making the children work hard.
c) making the children get good examination results.
d) becoming a head of department.

10 The speaker's general attitude to teaching is that
a) there are two ways but his is right and the other is wrong.
b) there are two ways and he uses both at different times.
c) there are two ways; his way is the best one to help him fulfil his personal ambition.
d) there are a lot of different ways for different kinds of pupils.

Practice unit 1.3

Read this text slowly and carefully (preferably twice, the first time for a general impression and the second time to study the details). Then answer the questions that follow.

I re-run the replica hijack

A week ago today a young Iranian hijacked a British Airways One Eleven flying from Manchester to Heathrow. He was using a metal replica gun which could just as easily have been real.

To check out the new and exciting security system introduced with much self con-   5
gratulation by British Airways over the last few days, I flew from Heathrow to
Manchester and back yesterday.

On each flight I carried two 'guns' – an expensive collector's replica of a Walther PPK
automatic, made of metal and identical in every respect to the real thing, and a 25p
plastic pistol bought from Woolworth's in Holborn on Friday.

In case metal detectors were in use (they weren't) I packed the gun in tissue paper   10
inside a new metal coffee pot I had been given for Christmas. That I packed in a briefcase along with some dirty laundry.

The idea was that if metal showed up on any detector I would produce the coffee pot
and hope the tissue paper would remain untouched. The plastic gun I stuffed inside my
bikini-style underpants; the resulting bulge emphasised my virility but didn't look   15
too obscenely obvious.

I killed a happy half hour at Heathrow before check-in time wandering round the book-
stalls, looking for toy guns and asking for books on hijacking. They hadn't any; a kindly
sales lady recommended Agatha Christie's 'Passenger to Frankfurt' but it was out of stock.

A disastrously slow, bad, and expensive breakfast enabled me to throw a calculated   20
tantrum shouting that if security was as bad as the service, then anyone could hijack
a plane any time they wished. No response.

So to Securicor. A half-hearted search of my two briefcases. No attempt to open the
coffee pot. Body search from a young man whom I deliberately upset by the subtle use

of psychological warfare – 'Give us a kiss, love,' I demanded as he reached gingerly up   25
my inside leg. After that he was in no mood to proceed farther.

Once BA4064 to Manchester was safely in the air I took myself off to the loo and retrieved
the guns. I walked back to my aisle seat 11c with the guns concealed as best I could in my hands.

For the rest of the flight I sat with them half-hidden in my lap, reading an American
paperback, *The Fall of a President*, by the staff of the *Washington Post*. Luckily the seats   30
next to mine were empty and no one paid any attention to me.

At Manchester I had a quick coffee and caught the same One Eleven (now called
BA4069) back. This time I had a nasty moment with Securicor. The baggage lady took
the coffee pot from my briefcase, opened it and removed the first few wads of tissue
paper, then she got bored and replaced them.   35

Had she continued she would have found my Walther automatic. Body search again
half-hearted and searcher again thrown by my merry cry of 'Give us a kiss, love' at the
crucial moment.

Another nasty incident when a chap who looked like a plain-clothed cop, and who had
flown out with me, accosted me boarding the plane. But he was just being friendly.   40

He had had to drop some papers in Manchester and come straight back and assumed
I was doing the same. Wasn't it a bore? Oh yes! Except that I was sitting on aisle seat 12d,
the return flight was a rerun of the outward journey.

The secretary of BALPA's (the pilots' trade union) security committee, Mr Gordon
Hurley, told me last night that the news of my trip was 'absolutely startling and   45
extremely frightening for pilots who had expected better security.'

At his request I am forwarding my report to BALPA which plans to raise it with the
Government's National Aviation Security Council as a matter of urgency. British Airways told me they were 'investigating the circumstances' but I would hear no more
from them for reasons of security.   50

The Department of Trade said last night it was 'seriously disturbed' by my journey
and had ordered an immediate investigation. 'It shows that security arrangements are
still not perfect,' a spokesman said. 'Every passenger on internal flights will now be
thoroughly searched even if it means more inconvenience and delays.'

Securicor admitted that their searches were not 100 per cent effective but they were   55
'doing their best.' The company wondered whether trips like mine were counter-
productive because they drew attention to weak spots.

At the end of a flight it is usual for pilots to wish passengers a safe journey. My pilot
both ways was a Captain Armstrong. I wish him safe journeys in future. But unless
security is tightened on internal flights I wouldn't bank on it.   60

Report in *The Guardian* by John Torode

Exercise

Choose the best answer to each question.

1   The purpose of the author's flight to Manchester and back was
a) to try to hijack a plane.
b) to see if the security system was as efficient as the airline said.
c) to deliver some papers.
d) to try to smuggle some guns through the customs.

2   He took
a) one real gun and one toy gun.
b) a real gun and a collector's replica.

c) two toy guns.
d) two different kinds of imitation gun.

3   He put one gun inside a coffee pot because
a) this would make it invisible to a metal detector.
b) a person looking for guns would get bored before looking in the coffee pot.
c) the dirty laundry in the briefcase would put the security guards off, so that they would not look carefully at the coffee pot.
d) the coffee pot would provide an explanation if the security guards used a machine which showed that he had metal in his luggage.

4   He put the plastic gun
a) inside the clothes he was wearing.
b) inside the dirty laundry in his briefcase.
c) in the coffee pot.
d) in his bikini.

5   Before getting on the plane at Heathrow
a) he tried to talk to people about security.
b) he tested the airport facilities.
c) his happy half hour was spoilt because he could not buy what he wanted.
d) he tried to draw attention to himself.

6   He prevented the security guards at Heathrow and Manchester from finding one of his guns by
a) throwing a tantrum.
b) behaving like a homosexual.
c) kissing them.
d) making them laugh.

7   During the flight he
a) hid the guns.
b) carried them openly.
c) half-hid them.
d) used a book to hide them.

8   On the return flight he travelled by
a) the same plane, with the same captain, but a different flight number; he sat in the same seat.
b) a different plane of the same type, but with the same captain; he sat in a different place.
c) the same plane, with the same flight number and crew; he sat in a different seat.
d) the same plane with the same captain, but a new flight number; he sat in a different seat.

9   Securicor is
a) a secret anti-hijacker organization.
b) a company that provides security guards.
c) another word for the customs.
d) a branch of the police.

10   Why did the other man accost the narrator at Manchester airport, according to the text?
a) He was bored.
b) He was friendly.
c) He was a policeman, but not in uniform, and suspected the narrator.
d) He was a policeman, but not in uniform; he did not suspect the narrator.

11 In the expression 'Wasn't it a bore?' (line 42), 'it' refers to
a) air travel.
b) having to make a return journey just to deliver papers.
c) Manchester.
d) the security precautions.

12 'A rerun of the outward journey' (line 43) means
a) exactly the same as the flight to Manchester.
b) like a flight abroad.
c) just as frightening as the first trip.
d) quite different from the journey from Heathrow.

13 The narrator reports the reactions of the pilots' union to his trip. They were
a) very upset.
b) not prepared to comment for security reasons.
c) planning to investigate.
d) critical of the narrator.

14 He also reports the reactions of other organizations. How many?
a) one
b) two
c) three
d) four

15 Securicor
a) promised to improve their security measures.
b) said that searches led to delays.
c) agreed that the narrator's trip might have been useful in showing up weaknesses.
d) felt that his trip might help future hijackers.

16 The result of the experiment was
a) to encourage a young Iranian to hijack a plane.
b) to show that trips of this kind were counter-productive.
c) to show that security precautions in British airports were not perfect.
d) to cause a lot more inconvenience and delays to passengers.

Teaching unit 2: Guessing unknown words

In any comprehension exam, the texts will contain words that you do not know. As you will not be allowed to use a dictionary, you will have to do your best to guess the meaning. It is important not to panic: even if there are fifteen or twenty words that you do not know, you should be able to understand most of them if you keep calm and think carefully. The main thing is to look at the *context* of each word – the sentence that it is in, and the sentences that come before and after. This will usually help you to get an idea of the meaning. (And look to see if the word is repeated later in the text; the more often it is used, the easier it is to understand.)

Unless your English is very good, you probably do not know the words 'dipstick' or 'stoat'. As long as they are alone, there is no way of guessing what they mean, but see what happens when they are put into a context:

a) *The car was making a funny noise, so I got out, opened the bonnet, and took out the dipstick to check the oil level.*

b) I heard a noise like a rabbit being killed by a stoat.

It is not very difficult to guess that a dipstick is the metal rod that is used for measuring the oil level in a car engine, or that a stoat is probably some kind of aggressive animal (even if you cannot tell exactly what).

Some words can be guessed from looking at their form. For instance, you may never have seen 'unforeseeable' before, but the different parts of the word – *un, fore, see, able* – should each tell you something and help you to guess the meaning. What do you think 'discontinuous' and 'preselect' mean? What about '*inky* black' and '*wavy* hair'?

Do not expect to be able to guess all the new words in a text. There will be some that you can only get a vague idea of, and others will be impossible. Do not waste time worrying about these: the most important thing is to understand the text as a whole as well as possible, and one or two difficult words will not make much difference.

Exercise a

You probably do not know many of these words: ungainly, boorish, knoll, tacky, shamble, undercoat, glum, notch, washer, gullible.

Look at the way they are used in the following sentences and then say, or write, what you think they might mean. (Do not look in your dictionary, of course.)

1   She's a big ungainly girl – always breaking things and falling over.
2   I've never met anybody as boorish as you are – what you said to me yesterday was absolutely unforgivable.
3   Napoleon rode up on to a little knoll to see the battle more clearly.
4   Put the glue on the broken pieces, wait until it is tacky and then stick them together.
5   He must be tired: look at the way he's shambling along.
6   I can't get on with painting the bathroom until the undercoat's dry.
7   You're looking a bit glum – what's the matter?
8   California Pete had thirty-four notches on his gun: one for each sheriff he had killed.
9   I think we need a new washer. The tap keeps dripping.
10 She's amazingly gullible. I told her yesterday that Switzerland had declared war on China and she believed every word.

Exercise b

Read the following text slowly and carefully without a dictionary, and without asking any questions. Then write down all the words and expressions in italics, and any others that you do not know. Look carefully at the context of each unknown word or expression, and write down what you think it might mean.

Drumming

Drumming is what you might call basic burglary*. You pick a *dead gaff* – a house you know or think is empty – sound the drum by knocking at the front door to make sure, stroll round the back, get in through a window and *turn the place over*.

The average suburban house is *a pushover* to enter. You don't need to carry any tools.

. . . Joe worked to an unvarying schedule. Once inside, he bolted all doors, leaving one   5
ground-floor window open, thus, like a wise general, securing his retreat. It seldom took

* *burglary*: stealing things from houses

him more than five minutes to go through the house. He took only easily portable stuff, jewellery, ornaments, cash, if there was any; he seldom bothered with clothes unless there was an exceptionally good fur coat.

He would leave by the front door, taking his time and emerging hat in hand, still 10 carrying on an imaginary conversation, for the benefit of passers-by. Little details that the average *drummer* never bothered about were very important to him. Never wear your hat while moving about in a strange house...

For the most part my job was to sit in the front room and keep my eyes glued to the gate while Joe turned over upstairs. This gave us an extra few seconds in which *to take stoppo* 15 if the householder did come back while we were still on the premises.

Joe used to maintain that there was no reason why *a two-handed team* of drummers should ever get *nicked*. He may have been right at that. He and I *grafted* together for the best part of four years and though we had some *narrow squeaks* we never got *pinched*. A lot of the time we were drumming three times a week, changing our *manor* each time, averaging 20 between thirty and fifty pounds a week.

From 'Changes in the Organisation of Thieving' by Mary McIntosh

Practice unit 2.1

Read each text carefully, without a dictionary, and then answer the questions that follow. While reading, pay special attention to the words that you do not know: look carefully at the context and see if you can get an idea of what they mean.

First passage

Hamburgers and Hamlet

Stratford-on-Avon, as we all know, has only one industry – Will Shakespeare – but there are two distinctly separate and increasingly hostile branches. There is the Royal Shakespeare Company, which presents superb productions of the plays at the Shakespeare Memorial Theatre on the Avon. And there are the townsfolk who largely live off the tourists who come, not to see the plays, but to gawk at Anne Hathaway's 5 Cottage, Shakespeare's birthplace and the other sights.

The worthy burghers of Stratford doubt that the theatre adds a penny to their revenue. They frankly dislike the RSC's actors, them with their long hair and beards and sandals and roistering habits. It's all deliciously ironic when you consider that Shakespeare, who earns their living, was himself an actor (with a beard) and did his share of roistering. 10

The tourist streams are not entirely separate. The sightseers who come by bus – and often take in Warwick Castle and Blenheim Palace on the side – don't usually see the plays, and some of them are even surprised to find a theatre in Stratford. However, the playgoers do manage a little sight-seeing along with their playgoing. It is the playgoers, the RSC contends, who bring in much of the town's revenue because they spend the night (some 15 of them four or five nights) pouring cash into the hotels and restaurants. The sightseers can take in everything and get out of town by nightfall.

The townsfolk don't see it this way and the borough council does not contribute directly to the subsidy of the Royal Shakespeare Company. Stratford cries poor traditionally. Nevertheless every hotel in town seems to be adding a new wing or cocktail lounge. 20

Hilton is building its own hotel there, which you may be sure will be adorned with Hamlet Hamburger Bars, the Lear Lounge, the Banquo Banqueting Room, and so forth, and will be very expensive.

 Anyway, the townsfolk can't understand why the Royal Shakespeare Company needs a subsidy. (The theatre has broken attendance records for three years in a row. Last year   25
its 1,431 seats were 94 per cent occupied all year long and this year they'll do better.) The reason, of course, is that costs have rocketed and ticket prices have stayed low.

 It would be a shame to raise prices too much because it would drive away the young people who are Stratford's most attractive clientele. They come entirely for the plays, not the sights. They all seem to look alike (though they come from all over) – lean,   30
pointed, dedicated faces, wearing jeans and sandals, munching their buns and bedding down for the night on the flagstones outside the theatre to buy the 20 seats and 80 standing-room tickets held for the sleepers and sold to them when the box office opens at 10.30 a.m.

From *The Observer*

Exercise a

Here are twelve words and expressions from the text. Each one is followed by four explanations of its meaning: only one is correct. Write down the numbers of the words and expressions, followed by the letters of the correct definitions. (For example, if you think 'gawk' means 'laugh', write 1a). Do this exercise without a dictionary.

1 *gawk* (line 5)
a) laugh
b) stare
c) point cameras
d) throw stones

2 *worthy* (line 7)
a) respectable
b) rich
c) valuable
d) talkative

3 *roistering* (lines 9, 10)
a) talking intelligently
b) sleeping
c) living wildly
d) acting

4 *revenue* (lines 7, 15)
a) taxes
b) price
c) income
d) value

5 *take in* (lines 12, 17)
a) visit
b) photograph
c) understand
d) pay for

6 *contends* (line 15)
a) denies
b) argues
c) doubts
d) hopes

7 *subsidy* (lines 19, 25)
a) financial support
b) collapse
c) idea
d) reputation

8 *cries poor* (line 19)
a) claims to be poor
b) is hard to poor people
c) takes no interest in Shakespeare
d) is not rich

9 *rocketed* (line 27)
a) been raised dishonestly
b) changed
c) gone up fast
d) stayed the same

10 *lean* (line 30)
a) sideways
b) tired
c) thin
d) foreign

11 *munching* (line 31)
a) selling
b) buying
c) stealing
d) eating

12 *flagstones* (line 32)
a) the stones that hold the flags
b) benches
c) pavement
d) pebbles

Second passage

A car chase

Bond reached under the dashboard and from its concealed holster drew out the long-barrelled ·45 Colt Army Special and laid it on the seat beside him. The battle was now in the open and somehow the Mercedes must be stopped.

Using the road as if it was Donington, Bond rammed his foot down and kept it there. Gradually, with the needle twitching either side of the hundred mark he began to narrow the gap.

Drax took the left-hand fork at Charing and hissed up the long hill. Ahead, in the giant

5

beam of his headlights, one of Bowaters' huge eight-wheeled AEC Diesel carriers was just grinding into the first bend of the hairpin, labouring under the fourteen tons of newsprint it was taking on a night run to one of the East Kent newspapers.   10

Drax cursed under his breath as he saw the long carrier with the twenty gigantic rolls, each containing five miles of newsprint, roped to its platform. Right in the middle of the tricky S-bend at the top of the hill.

He looked in the driving mirror and saw the Bentley coming into the fork.

And then Drax had his idea.   15

'Krebs,' the word was a pistol shot. 'Get out your knife.'

There was a sharp click and the stiletto was in Krebs's hand. One didn't dawdle when there was that note in the master's voice.

'I am going to slow down behind this lorry. Take your shoes and socks off and climb out on to the bonnet and when I come up behind the lorry jump on to it. I shall be going   20 at walking-pace. It will be safe. Cut the ropes that hold the rolls of paper. The left ones first. Then the right. I shall have pulled up level with the lorry and when you have cut the second lot jump into the car. Be careful you are not swept off with the paper.'

Drax dowsed his headlights and swept round the bend at eighty. The lorry was twenty yards ahead and Drax had to brake hard to avoid crashing into its tail. The Mercedes exe-   25 cuted a dry skid until its radiator was almost underneath the platform of the carrier.

Drax changed down to second. 'Now!' He held the car steady as a rock as Krebs, with bare feet, went over the windscreen and scrambled along the shining bonnet, his knife in his hand.

With a leap he was up and hacking at the left-hand ropes. Drax pulled away to the right 30 and crawled up level with the rear wheels of the Diesel, the oily smoke from its exhaust in his eyes and nostrils.

Bond's lights were just showing round the bend.

There was a series of huge thuds as the left-hand rolls poured off the back of the lorry into the road and went hurtling off into the darkness. And more thuds as the right- 35 hand ropes parted. One roll burst as it landed and Drax heard a tearing rattle as the un-winding paper crashed back down the one-in-ten gradient.

Released of its load the lorry almost bounded forward and Drax had to accelerate a little to catch the flying figure of Krebs who landed half across Gala's back and half in the front seat. Drax stamped his foot into the floor and sped off up the hill, ignoring a   40 shout from the lorry-driver above the clatter of the Diesel pistons as he shot ahead.

As he hurtled round the next bend he saw the shaft of two headlights curve up into the sky above the tops of the trees until they were almost vertical. They wavered there for an instant and then the beams whirled away across the sky and went out.

A great barking laugh broke out of Drax as for a split second he took his eyes off the 45 road and raised his face triumphantly towards the stars.

From *Moonraker* by Ian Fleming

Exercise b

Choose the best answer to each question.

1   Which is true?
a) Bond, driving a Bentley, is chasing Drax, who is driving a Mercedes.
b) Bond, driving a Mercedes, is chasing Drax, who is driving a Bentley.
c) Drax, driving a Bentley, is chasing Bond, who is driving a Mercedes.
d) Drax, driving a Mercedes, is chasing Bond, who is driving a Bentley.

2   What weapon did Bond take out?
a) a gun from under the seat
b) an army knife from a hidden pocket
c) a gun which was hidden in the front of the car
d) a special army machine for stopping cars

3   What do you think Donington is (line 4)?
a) a town
b) a country road
c) a main road
d) a race-track

4   'Bond rammed his foot down and kept it there' (line 4). This expression shows
a) that he found it difficult to stay in his seat on the rough road.
b) that he was feeling nervous.
c) that he was very sure of himself.
d) that he wanted to drive fast.

5   What do you think 'newsprint' is (line 9)?
a) newspapers
b) paper for printing newspapers
c) posters to advertise newspapers
d) wrapping paper

6   What is 'dawdle' (line 17)?
a) complain
b) go slowly
c) hurry
d) disagree violently

7   'Dowsed' (line 24) means
a) switched on
b) switched off
c) checked
d) used

8   'Hacking' (line 30) means
a) cutting
b) pulling
c) looking
d) working

9   The scene of the story is
a) a long hill with a bend at each end.
b) a steep gradient with a lot of bends.
c) a long steep hill with a double bend at the top.
d) a hairpin bend, followed by a one-in-ten gradient.

10 By cutting the rolls of newsprint, Drax and Krebs
a) stop Bond.
b) cause Bond to crash into the lorry.
c) slow Bond down.
d) cause the lorry to crash.

Practice unit 2.2

Read each text carefully, without a dictionary, and then answer the questions that follow. While reading, pay special attention to the words that you do not know: look carefully at the context and see if you can get an idea of what they mean.

First passage

Bat Dongin

Bat Dongin was a professional gunthrower the Moore boys brought in to kill Maurice Hanline. The Moore boys – Hogger, Fred, and Shorty – owned most of the town and most of the land around it, except the Hanline place. The Moore boys had decided they would be able to deal better with the new owner of the Hanline place after she had been made a widow. Shorty Moore would have killed Hanline himself, but the older, wiser   5
brothers wanted the land deal to be clean so they brought in Bat Dongin.

Fort Hill was the centre for butchering buffalo that year, and wherever the buffalo butchers were working for steady money, thugs and riffraff skulked in. There were about four thousand people in the town. Sometimes cowhands rode through. If they were sober they generally kept on riding. Soldiers, horse thieves, lost women, cow   10
thieves, and back-shooters were most of Fort Hill that season when the buffalo were being diminished to extinction. Outside of maybe one hundred and ten people, the town was a mongrel's vomit.

The fort itself was up on the bluff. So was the big mercantile store. The tang of the town was down under the bluff in the flats, where every building was noisy and fancy   15
and where the Moore boys owned four of the seven honkatonks. It was no place to go unarmed or to walk in the dark. The moon never seemed to come out over Fort Hill. The whisky didn't taste right. A man could strike a wooden match on the cheeks of most of the drunken dance-hall women while they slept and never wake them. About daylight any morning, anyone who took a stroll down by the river might find another body   20
hanging by its neck from a cotton-wood tree with a sign stuck on it that said *Horse Thief No. 24* or whatever number it happened to be.

The Moore boys' biggest saloon was called The Jefferson House. It was painted red and had gilt porch posts and gold swinging doors. All drinks and seegars were two bits apiece. In front of it drunken Indians staggered around or lay face down in the mud. The thugs   25
who called themselves buffalo hunters would sit on the front gallery to insult any woman who walked past. Inside, any kind of game any customer wanted to play was available - keno, chuckaluck, roulette, Spanish monte, poker, faro, casino – anything at all. The price of buffalo hides* had dropped to sixty cents. The tramp buffalo butchers were feeling hollow. Most of them were on foot. They'd kill a man for a horse or five dollars.   30
They were not only evil and mean, they smelled bad. The whole town stank. Wagon trains were carrying buffalo hides out but acres of ground all around the town were still covered and reeking with them.

Bat Dongin came into The Jefferson House late in the afternoon and ordered himself a heavy dinner. He had been told that Maurice Hanline would come in at nine o'clock.   35
Waiting made him nervous. Dongin was a skinny man with a strong sour smell and a port-wine scar on the left side of his face from hairline to jawline. He whined everything

* *hides*: skins

he said. By seven o'clock he was catching cards behind a rank cigar in Major Patten's
poker game with three other players: Tom Pryor, the town printer; Hogger Moore;
and Frank O'Connell, the lawyer who had come to the town travelling for Mooney &   40
Schmidt, the fancy-food firm.

From *A Talent for Loving* by Richard Condon

Exercise a

Choose the best answer to each question.

1 Why did the Moore boys want Maurice Hanline killed?
a) Because he was an enemy of Shorty's.
b) Because he would not let his wife sell them the land.
c) Because they needed his land to add to their property.
d) Because he was too honest.

2 Why did they not want Shorty to kill him?
a) They were afraid of being found out.
b) Shorty was too young.
c) Bat Dongin was a professional, so he would do the job better.
d) They thought it was better if the murder was done by somebody not involved in
buying Hanline's property.

3 Why were there so many bad characters in the town?
a) Because thugs and riffraff skulked in.
b) Because of the Moore boys.
c) They were attracted by the money that the buffalo-butchers brought in.
d) Because of all the saloons.

4 What do you think 'thugs and riffraff' (line 8) means?
a) criminals and people with bad reputations
b) dance-hall women
c) horse thieves
d) buffalo butchers

5 A 'mongrel' is a dog of mixed parentage. What do you think the 'one hundred and
ten people' (line 12) were?
a) the worst people in Fort Hill
b) the best people in Fort Hill
c) buffalo hunters
d) the people who worked for the Moore family

6 Do you think a 'bluff' (line 15) is
a) a kind of lie
b) a kind of hill
c) a kind of card game
d) a forest

7 What are 'honkatonks' (line 16)?
a) houses for drinking, dancing and gambling
b) small mercantile stores
c) stables
d) shops

8   Why was a buffalo butcher ready to kill people?
a) He could not earn enough money for his work.
b) His work made him hard and aggressive.
c) He needed money for drink and gambling.
d) If he could steal five dollars from his victim, he could buy a horse with it.

9   What do you think 'reeking' means (line 33)?
a) piled
b) shining
c) looking unpleasant
d) smelling bad

10 Bat Dongin went to the Jefferson House because he wanted to
a) have dinner.
b) play cards.
c) shoot Maurice Hanline.
d) forget his nervousness.

Second passage

Guidance on buying accessories

It seems best to approach the subject by dividing *accessories* into rough groups. First are items that may be considered essential from the safety point of view. I should not, for instance, like to own a car without a *rear screen heater*, and though many models now offer these as standard equipment, where one is not fitted the investment of £5 or so is well worth it.

For small children, a special safety seat is a 'must'; the number of *toddlers* travelling *untethered* in cars, particularly in front seats, is horrifying. Supplementary lights – for fog, reversing and so on – are also important for safety. Outside mirrors (wing or door, there are arguments both ways) are in my view indispensable, though they are still not a legal requirement.

Correct tyre pressures are another vital safety factor, and garage pumps cannot always be relied on. In any case it is better to check pressures before starting off when the tyres are still cold. A foot pump can still be bought for as little as £2, while a *pressure gauge* costs a mere 40p or so. A battery charger is a useful precautionary item: *Wipac do one*, the Chargemobile Chief, which can be installed under the bonnet.

Emergency equipment for carrying in the car must include a first-aid kit, a set of basic tools (notably screw-drivers and spanners), a replacement windscreen, *tow-rope*, and red warning triangle. The last is compulsory in many Continental countries. Most of these items can be bought from the Automobile Association, also an inspection light, which works off the car battery, and a 24-piece socket set for getting at nuts the spanner cannot reach. To meet another kind of crisis, Gunson's automatic petrol reserve tank, approved by the AA and with anti-theft device, is available at £7.90 plus value-added tax.

A *roof-rack* is more useful than it might seem. It may carry the family luggage to the seaside only once a year, but there are many other long loads that will not go inside the car like planks, a carpet, and even small trees. *Boot racks* have their uses, too, as long as the load does not block the view through the rear window.

Car care products include anti-freeze, screen wash, de-icers, rust repair kits and *touch-up paint*. I suspect that a lot less touching up would be necessary if motorists spent

5

10

15

20

25

25p or so on a pair of *car door buffers*. There is some argument about the best preparations for cleaning the car, particularly the merits of shampoos, but no dispute that mud and   30
dirt *lodged in crevices* is a sure means of encouraging corrosion. Here a brush can be invaluable; indeed, to clean a car thoroughly two or three of different size and stiffness are probably necessary.

From *The Times*

Exercise b

After reading the whole passage carefully, write down the following words and expressions (they are printed in italics in the text), and write short simple explanations of what you think they might mean.

accessories   rear screen heater   toddlers   untethered   pressure gauge
Wipac do one   tow-rope   roof-rack   boot racks   touch-up paint
car door buffers   lodged in crevices

Practice unit 2.3

Read the text carefully, without a dictionary, and then answer the questions that follow. While reading, pay special attention to the words that you do not know: look carefully at the context and see if you can get an idea of what they mean.

Pitying animals

Now which are the animals really to be pitied in captivity? I have already given a partial answer to this question: In the first place, those clever and highly developed beings whose lively mentality and urge for activity can find no outlet behind the bars of the cage. Furthermore, all those animals which are ruled by strong drives that cannot be satisfied in captivity. This is most conspicuous, even for the uninitiated, in the case of animals   5
which, when living in a free state, are accustomed to roam about widely and therefore have a correspondingly strong drive for locomotion. Owing to this frustrated desire, foxes and wolves housed, in many old-fashioned zoos, in cages which are far too small, are among the most pitiable of all caged animals.

   Another piteous scene, seldom noticed by ordinary zoo visitors, is enacted by some   10
species of swans at migration time. These creatures, like most other water fowl, are in zoos generally rendered incapable of flight by the operation of 'pinioning', that is the amputation of the wing bone at the metacarpal joint. The birds never really grasp that they can fly no more and they try again and again. I do not like pinioned water birds; the missing tip of one wing and the still sadder picture that the bird makes when it   15
spreads its wings spoil most of my pleasure in it, even if it belongs to one of those species which do not suffer mentally by the mutilation.

   Though pinioned swans generally seem happy and signify their contentment, under proper care, by hatching and rearing their young without any trouble, at migration time things become different: the swans repeatedly swim to the lee side of the pond, in order   20
to have the whole extent of its surface at their disposal when trying to take off against the wind. All the while, their sonorous flying calls can be heard as they try to rise, and again and again the grand preparations end in a pathetic flutter of the one and half wings; a truly sorry picture!

But of all animals that suffer under the inefficient methods of many zoological   25
gardens, by far the most unfortunate are those mentally alert creatures of whom we have
spoken above. These, however, rarely awaken the pity of the zoo visitor, least of all
when such an originally highly intelligent animal has deteriorated, under the influence
of close confinement, into a crazy idiot, a very caricature of its former self. I have never
heard an exclamation of sympathy from the onlookers in the parrot house. Sentimental   30
old ladies, the fanatical sponsors of the Societies for Prevention of Cruelty to Animals,
have no compunction in keeping a grey parrot or cockatoo in a relatively small cage or
even chained to a perch. Now these larger species of the parrot tribe are not only clever
but mentally and bodily uncommonly vivacious; and, together with the large corvines,
they are probably the only birds which can suffer from that state of mind, common to   35
prisoners, namely boredom. But nobody pities these pathetic creatures in their bell-shaped
cages of martyrdom. Uncomprehendingly, the fond owner imagines that the bird is
bowing, when it constantly repeats the bobbing head movements which, in reality, are
the stereotyped remnants of its desperate attempts to escape from its cage. Free such an
unhappy prisoner, and it will take weeks, even months, before it really dares to fly.   40

More wretched still in confinement are monkeys, above all the anthropoid apes. They
are the only captive animals which can derive serious bodily harm from their mental
suffering. Anthropoid apes can become literally bored to death, particularly when they are
kept alone in too small cages. For this and no other reason, it is easily explained why
monkey babies thrive admirably in private ownership where they 'live as the family',   45
but that they immediately begin to pine when, having become too large and dangerous,
they are transferred to the cages of the nearest zoo. My capuchin monkey Gloria was
overtaken by this fate. It is no exaggeration when I say that real success in the keeping of
anthropoid apes was only achieved when it was realized how to prevent the mental
sufferings caused by confinement. I have beside me the wonderful chimpanzee book   50
by Robert Yerkes, one of the best authorities on this kind of ape; from this work it may
be concluded that mental hygiene plays just as important a role as physical, in the main-
tenance of health of these most human of all animals. On the other hand, to keep anthropoid apes in solitary confinement and in such small cages as are still to be found in many
zoos, is an act of cruelty which should be punishable by law.   55

In his big anthropoid ape station in Orange Park, Florida, Yerkes has kept, for many
years, a chimpanzee colony, which has multiplied freely and in which the apes live as
happily as do my lesser whitethroats in their aviary, and much more happily than you or I.

From *King Solomon's Ring* by Konrad Lorenz

Exercise

Choose the best answer to each question.

1 What is an 'outlet' (line 3)?
a) an opportunity for expression
b) a way out
c) a chance of escape
d) an exit

2 What does 'the uninitiated' mean (line 5)?
a) people who visit zoos
b) people who do not like animals
c) people who have no special knowledge
d) people who do not visit zoos

3   What do you think 'roam' (line 6) means?
a) hunt
b) wander
c) fight
d) run very fast

4   According to the author, what kind of animals suffer most in captivity?
a) hunting animals
b) parrots
c) swans and apes
d) animals which have needs that cannot be satisfied in cages

5   What exactly is 'pinioning' (line 12)?
a) putting birds in cages
b) cutting off a bird's wing
c) tying a bird's wing
d) cutting off part of a bird's wing

6   What do you think 'hatching and rearing their young' (line 19) means?
a) raising families
b) getting on well with smaller birds
c) behaving like young birds
d) attacking smaller birds

7   Which is the 'lee side' of the pond (line 20)?
a) the side the wind is blowing from
b) the side which is sheltered from the wind
c) the side the wind is blowing towards
d) the side where the water is highest

8   According to the author, swans in captivity are
a) happy unless their wings have been cut.
b) happy most of the time, but unhappy at a certain season of the year.
c) unhappy most of the time.
d) only happy when they are bringing up families.

9   The word 'very', in line 29 ('a very caricature'), means
a) extremely
b) real
c) changed
d) mostly

10 What effect does confinement have on clever animals, according to the text?
a) They never stop trying to escape.
b) They lose all their energy.
c) They become unhygienic.
d) They may go mad or die.

11 What does 'sponsors' (line 31) mean, in your opinion?
a) enemies
b) attackers
c) admirers
d) supporters

12 In line 32, the expression 'have no compunction about' occurs. Do you think this means
a) have no reaction to
b) have no understanding of
c) do not feel bad about
d) are delighted to

13 What does the author say about sentimental old ladies?
a) They do not care about animals.
b) They hate making animals suffer.
c) They enjoy making animals suffer.
d) They do not realise how they make animals suffer.

14 What do you think 'large corvines' are (line 34)?
a) another kind of bird
b) another kind of parrot
c) hunting animals
d) anthropoid apes

15 What about 'stereotyped' (line 39)?
a) violent
b) mechanically repeated
c) shown in a picture
d) accompanied by sound

16 'Wretched' (line 41) means
a) happy
b) unhappy
c) apathetic
d) desperate

17 The reaction of a caged parrot to freedom, according to the text, is that
a) it cannot fly any more.
b) it does not want to leave its cage.
c) it is afraid to fly.
d) it flies away at once.

18 'Thrive' (line 45) means
a) learn to move
b) grow big
c) are happy and healthy
d) get on well with people

19 'Pine' (line 46) means
a) get violent
b) become sick and unhappy
c) go mad
d) cause trouble

20 According to the author, the main problem about keeping apes in zoos is that
a) zoos are not usually clean anough.
b) zoos are too impersonal.
c) zoos often put apes alone in small cages, which causes them physical and mental suffering.
d) apes can only be happy when they are brought up in private ownership where they
'live as the family'.

Teaching unit 3: Understanding complicated sentences 1

What makes a text difficult to understand? It is not always because the ideas are difficult to follow, or because the writer uses unusual words. Sometimes a very simple argument or description can become much more difficult to read just because of the way the sentences are constructed.

Look at these four sentences:

There were some people sitting at the next table.
Mary was busily engaged in giving her opinion of what was wrong with them.
John told Mary that he was going to leave the restaurant if she went on talking like that.
He was becoming more and more ill at ease and embarrassed.

Now look at a different way of presenting the same facts:

John, who was becoming more and more ill at ease and embarrassed, told Mary, who was busily engaged in giving her opinion of what was wrong with the people sitting at the next table, that if she went on talking like that he was going to leave the restaurant.

What exactly has happened? One part of the third sentence (*John told Mary that he was going to leave the restaurant*) has been used as a sort of box, and everything else has been put inside it. The different parts of the 'box'-sentence (*John, told Mary, that,* and *he was going to leave the restaurant*) have been separated from each other, so that it is not easy at first to see the connections between them, and the sentence becomes harder to follow.

Here is a more difficult example:

Any member who has not paid his subscription by the end of the month following the month in which his subscription becomes due for payment shall, unless he has been previously exempted from payment under rule 16, or unless he can show good reason why his subscription should not be paid, be expelled from the club.

Exercise a

Read the following short texts and answer the questions that come after them.

The intention of other people concerned, such as the Minister of Defence, to influence the government leaders to adapt their policy to fit in with the demands of the right wing, cannot be ignored.

1   What is the subject of 'cannot be ignored'?
a) the intention
b) other people concerned
c) the Minister of Defence
d) the demands of the right wing

2   The intention of other people concerned is
a) to influence the government leaders.
b) to adapt their policy.
c) to fit in with the wishes of the right wing.
d) that they should not be ignored.

One way of deciding what to do when you have difficulty in choosing the best course of action is to toss a coin.

3   What is the subject of the verb 'is'?

So although the weather was very changeable, and in some cases caused us serious inconvenience, on the whole our holiday, which we had planned in great detail several months before, turned out to be satisfactory.

4 This sentence consists of a basic sentence of seven words, to which all the rest has been added afterwards. Can you write the basic sentence?

Arthur was not sure which way to go, for he had been left alone by his friends, and, when an old man came along the road accompanied by a little boy, said 'Excuse me, sir'.

5 Who said 'Excuse me, sir'?

The really important point is that because he did not invite the one man he certainly should have asked his father was furious.

6 Who was furious?
7 Does the text say that he should have asked his father?

The quite unusual alarm with which Mrs Smith, who was generally quite a calm person, received the news of the change of plans convinced me that there must be something seriously wrong.

8 Who or what convinced me that there must be something seriously wrong?
a) Mrs Smith's alarm
b) Mrs Smith
c) the news of the change of plans
d) the change of plans

Relative structures

Sentences often become long and complicated because of the use of relative pronouns (who, which, etc.). Here is an example:

No one could have expected that this writer, who had spent more than half of his life attacking the cynical and self-interested way in which his country exploited its colonies, would change so far in his later years as to become a member of the government and a passionate supporter of colonialism.

There are two relative clauses, containing more than twenty words, between the principal subject ('this writer') and the beginning of its verb ('would'); this naturally makes the sentence less easy to understand at first reading.

The use of 'whose', or of prepositions with relative pronouns, can also make sentences difficult to read. Examples:

a) *Picasso was a painter whose importance to modern art cannot be overestimated.*
b) *There are some patients the seriousness of whose illnesses makes it impossible to treat them at home.*

Quite often we leave out relative pronouns in English, and this, too, can make a sentence difficult to understand.
Examples:

a) *The medicines she is being supplied with are very probably causing her actual harm. (= The medicines with which she is being supplied...)*
b) *The document I was asked to put my name on was a sort of contract. (= The document on which I was...)*

Another difficulty can be caused by the use of a participle (form in -ed or -ing) instead of a complete relative clause. (For example, 'The man questioned...' instead of 'The man who was questioned...') This can be confusing because some past participles, like 'questioned', look exactly like past tenses (so you might think at first that 'The man questioned' means 'The man asked somebody a question'.)

More examples:

a) *I am absolutely certain that a man called Joe Simons is responsible for the theft.*
b) *One of the visitors expected last week did not come.*

Exercise b

Read these texts and answer the questions that follow.

It must not be forgotten that the willingness with which a person will move from the house where he has lived all his life and settle in an old people's home is an important factor in planning for the aged.

1 What is an important factor?
a) the house where he has lived all his life
b) a person
c) the willingness with which a person will move
d) an old people's home

On the ship there was a millionaire, the exact size of whose fortune was a frequent subject of discussion among the other passengers.

2 Which noun is the subject of the second 'was'?
a) millionaire
b) size
c) fortune
d) discussion

The film she told me about and advised me to see when we met the other week at – I think – Celia's party turned out to be very dull.

3 What was dull? (Answer in two words.)

The rebel leader found out that in spite of the precautions of the soldiers he had bought the guns from the police had planted an informer among them.

4 Who had the rebel leader bought the guns from?

A number of the children asked for comments on the proposals to expel some immigrants told reporters that they disagreed.

5 Who disagreed?

Practice unit 3.1

Read the text slowly and carefully and then do the exercises that follow.

Invalid* tricycles

It is ironic that this Government which has done more than all its predecessors to remedy the shameful neglect of the disabled should have turned its back on the most glaring scandal of all. The problems of the disabled tricycle driver have been extensively publicised – some

* *invalid:* somebody who cannot walk or move normally because of an illness or injury

would argue too much so. But as a classic example of maladministration, in spite of the best of intentions, it is hard to beat.

For the past decade the poor design, discomfort, and dangerous handling characteristics of the invalid tricycle have never been out of the news. Report after report has found them to be so seriously wanting that if it had been a normal vehicle, the outcry would have been such as to cause an immediate halt in production and demands for a total recall.

In 1969 the Consumers' Association described the old model, of which there are still nearly 14,000 on the road, as 'disastrous vehicles.' It criticised them for being unstable, noisy, and for their almost total lack of crash protection. A follow-up report in 1972 on the improved Model 70, of which there are nearly seven thousand on the road, found that it was still unstable when cornering at speed, still extremely noisy, and still seriously lacking in safety features.

The validity of these criticisms was endorsed by independent tests conducted by the Cranfield Institute of Technology in July, 1973. The tricycle was reported to be seriously defective in braking, swerving, and wind gust tests. The Institute's director, Professor J. R. Ellis, was quoted as saying after the tricycle had been blown up to 14 feet from a straight course in a wind test: 'I would not have an invalid tricycle under any circumstances even if I became disabled. It is the only vehicle we have ever had at this place where we have had to break off tests because the test drivers were too frightened about the dangers of overturning.'

The dangers were not merely experienced on the test track. In March this year the Research Institute for Consumer Affairs analysed the experiences of 1,300 tricycle drivers.

Their letters made very unhappy reading. 'In practice,' said the Consumers' Association, 'the trikes disabled people are being supplied with are very often causing them anxiety, social deprivation, and all too often, actual injury. No vehicle should catch fire spontaneously; it is particularly horrifying that vehicles for the disabled do. Clearly the present tricycle is an unsatisfactory and hazardous vehicle.'

A feature of the tricycle which concerns disabled drivers just as keenly as safety, is its inability to carry a passenger. More than half of those who responded to the RICA survey complained of isolation and loneliness and the fear of being stranded alone in a broken-down vehicle.

In response to public concern, Mr Heath's Government asked Baroness Sharp, a former permanent secretary to the Ministry of Housing, to inquire into these criticisms. Her report, after a two-year investigation, was finally published in April this year. Its main finding was that 'the case for replacing the three wheeler by cars is overwhelming.'

This conclusion was inevitable if for no other reason than that the price of a specially adapted car was less than that of a tricycle. The Sharp report estimated that the average annual cost to the Government of providing, adapting, maintaining and insuring a small car was about £155, about £25 less than a three wheeler.

These costings underlined the infelicity – to use a mild word – of the Department of Health's position. It was (and still is) supplying a vehicle, significantly inferior in safety, comfort, design and performance to a small car, not because it is cheaper but because if it acted otherwise it would open the floodgates to public expenditure. For more than a decade what has prevented and still stands in the way of a rational solution is that the number of those eligible for an invalid tricycle far exceeds the number of those who actually apply. Thus Lady Sharp estimated that if the Department simply replaced tricycles with cars, the cost of the service might treble to £18 million.

The prospect then unless the Government thinks again is that the majority of the 21,000 invalid tricycles now on the road will continue to be there for the indefinite future.

Mr Harold Wilson summed up the situation all too clearly last October when in

Opposition: 'There is some anxiety about a suggestion', he said, 'that the Department's attitude to this question derives from a fear that if they were to accept the case for a car   55
which is more easy to control rather than less, with an equivalent standard of safety, comfort, and reliability to those of other small cars – and allegedly cheaper – then the demand for such a vehicle would considerably exceed the demands for the less satisfactory three wheeler. Then it would cost more, not because our vehicle costs more, but because more would be applied for. If that is the argument – and I can understand why no one   60
wants to make it articulate – it is unacceptable.'

Recent statistical evidence has confirmed that the tricycles are considerably less safe than cars. In the year ended September 1973, the Department of the Environment has disclosed that the rate of injury accidents per million miles was 5·88 for invalid tricycles, compared to only 1·53 for adapted cars used by the disabled. And in the year   65
ended September 1974, out of just over 6,500 Model 70 tricycles on the road, no less than 2,500 had been involved in accidents.

The starting point for any solution is to accept that the rights of the 20,000 drivers who now drive tricycles will have to be safeguarded. The vast majority will want to transfer to cars. They should be allowed to do so, either by cash grants or by supplying the   70
vehicles directly, on a phased basis, the speed of which will depend on the resources that can be made available. The Treasury should be urged to be generous, to permit this limited operation to be completed as soon as possible.

There will, of course, be a few tricycle drivers who will not want to switch. There will be also a few drivers, the nature of whose disability will make it difficult if not   75
impossible for them to drive a car. For these two groups some form of tricycle will have to continue in production, though there is a strong argument that future models should be substantially modified, and made much less powerful, possibly using electric motors.

From an article in *The Guardian* by Adam Raphael

Exercise a

Choose the best answer to each question.

1   The writer's main conclusion is that
a) there has been too much discussion of the dangers of invalid tricycles.
b) invalid tricycles should be replaced by cars as soon as possible.
c) it is not practicable to replace invalid tricycles by cars.
d) there is a great deal to be said on both sides.

2   According to the writer, the main argument for changing to cars is that
a) this would benefit a greater number of invalids.
b) cars are cheaper.
c) invalids could carry passengers.
d) cars are safer.

3   The main reason against changing to cars, according to the passage, is that
a) a car costs more than a tricycle.
b) many invalids would not want to change.
c) the Department of the Environment are against the change.
d) so many people would apply for cars that the government would have to find much more money.

4   The text refers to several different organisations. Which one apparently has a different attitude from the others?
a) the Consumers' Association
b) the Department of Health
c) the Department of the Environment
d) the Research Institute for Consumer Affairs

5   The expression 'unless the government thinks again' (line 51) means
a) if the government does not change its policy
b) if the government adopts a different policy
c) if the government asks for another report
d) if the government decides not to continue with its present attitude

6   When Harold Wilson summed up the situation 'all too clearly' (line 53), his point was that
a) the Department of Health were anxious about a suggestion that had been made.
b) the Department of the Environment had a negative attitude to the safety of invalid tricycles.
c) the Department of Health seemed to be afraid to replace tricycles by cars because of the cost.
d) the case for an improved car is unacceptable.

7   The Department of the Environment's statistics show that
a) in 1972–3 invalid tricycles were nearly four times as dangerous as ordinary cars.
b) in 1972–3 invalid tricycles were nearly four times as dangerous as cars used by invalids.
c) in 1972–3 over a third of invalid tricycles were involved in accidents.
d) in the period from September 1972 to September 1974, Model 70 tricycles had an accident record of 5·88 per 6,500 vehicles on the road.

8   What is meant by 'the number of those eligible for an invalid tricycle far exceeds the number of those who actually apply' (lines 47–9)?
a) More people ask for a tricycle than get one.
b) More people get a tricycle than ask for one.
c) Many people could have a tricycle but don't ask for one.
d) Many people ask for a tricycle who have no right to one.

9   The word 'some', in line 3, refers to
a) problems
b) disabled tricycle drivers
c) people in general
d) publications

10 The word 'it', in line 5, refers to
a) maladministration
b) the government
c) the government's attitude to disabled tricycle drivers
d) the shameful neglect of the disabled

11 The word 'its', in line 37, refers to
a) public concern
b) Baroness Sharp's report
c) the two-year investigation
d) Mr Heath's Government

12 In the sentence beginning 'It was (and still is) . . .' (line 44), the word 'it' occurs four times. What do you think these four uses of 'it' refer to?
a) the same thing each time
b) two different things
c) three different things
d) four different things

Exercise b: Same or different?

Write the numbers of the sentences, followed by S (if you think that the sentence says the same thing as the text) or D (if you think that the meaning is different).

1 According to the writer this government has neglected the disabled more than earlier governments. (1st paragraph)
2 The public has been told a lot about the disadvantages of invalid tricycles during the last ten years. (2nd paragraph)
3 These tricycles have been found to be as seriously defective as normal vehicles. (2nd paragraph)
4 There has been a public outcry about these vehicles. (2nd paragraph)
5 The Consumers' Association reported that two different models were dangerous. (3rd paragraph)
6 The Consumers' Association carried out independent tests at the Cranfield Institute of Technology which confirmed these criticisms. (4th paragraph)
7 Professor Ellis was blown a long way to the side in a test which he carried out. (4th paragraph)
8 Invalid tricycles can catch fire by themselves. (6th paragraph)
9 Disabled drivers are distressed because they cannot carry passengers in their tricycles. (7th paragraph)
10 Baroness Sharp, in recommending that tricycles should be replaced by cars, gave the difference in price as the only reason. (9th paragraph)

Practice unit 3.2

Read each text slowly and carefully and then answer the questions that follow.

First passage

The workhouse

What makes the hair stand on end even more than the harrowing tales of human need contained in this readable and impressively researched history of the workhouse, is that while that hated Victorian institution may have disappeared, together with the Poor Laws that created it, the attitudes behind them still exist and still dictate our policies towards the deprived.   5

Above all, there was and still is the belief that if the physically fit are poor it is because they are idle only from choice. As far back as the sixteenth century the law dictated: '*If any man or woman, able to work, should refuse to labour and live idly for three days, he or she should be branded with a red-hot iron on the breast with the letter " V" and should be the slave for two years of any person who should inform of such idler.*'   10

We may not brand the unemployed with a red-hot iron today, but sear their minds with criticism we do: the 'deserving' and 'undeserving' poor still exist. Thus it is easier for politicians to make provision for widows than for unmarried mothers, easier for charities to raise money for pets (apparently blameless for their needs) than for the homeless, the poor, or ex-prisoners. 15

The belief, belied by all the facts of economic life, that it is impossible to be poor and able-bodied unless you are feckless or idle leads to so-called 'relief' institutions that deliberately set out to deter custom. That was the concept of the workhouse. One of its pioneers wrote: 'I wish to see the workhouse looked to with dread by our labouring classes and the reproach for being an inmate of it extend downwards from father to son...Let 20 the poor see and feel that their parish, although it will not allow them to perish through absolute want, is yet the hardest taskmaster, the closest paymaster, and the most harsh and unkind friend they can apply to.'

Attitudes of the past? Not at all. Even today many local politicians and welfare officers will defend the punitive conditions of hostels for the homeless as a necessary incentive to 25 the homeless to find alternative accommodation – no matter that it is sheer lack of accommodation that makes them homeless in the first place.

It is shattering how the author's descriptions of the workhouse coincide with some hostels for the homeless that I have seen. 'The basic item of furniture was a cheap, wooden bed, with a mattress made of sacking and two or three blankets. Pillows were 30 "unnecessary" and sheets, if provided, were of the coarsest kind. Few people enjoyed the luxury of a single bed, and some beds, both single and double, were arranged in two tiers, like bunks in an army barrack room...The only decorations on the walls were the lists of regulations, enjoining instant obedience to the master...There were no news-papers, no books, and for the younger inmates no games and no toys. The children, 35 like their elders, fought, teased each other, threw stones, or most commonly, sat listlessly about, stupefied with boredom and apathy.'

Details of the past? Not at all. I have seen homeless families packed into one dormitory in conditions almost exactly the same.

From an article in *Punch* by Des Wilson

Exercise a

Choose the best answer to each question.

1 This passage seems to be taken from
a) a history book.
b) an article on the poor.
c) a book review.
d) an article on the workhouse.

2 The workhouse is/was
a) a Victorian hostel for the poor and homeless.
b) a prison.
c) a home for unmarried mothers, the homeless, the poor, and ex-prisoners.
d) a new type of hostel for people with nowhere to live.

3 What 'makes the hair stand on end' most of all, according to the author?
a) the harrowing tales of human need
b) the history of the workhouse
c) the fact that the workhouse has disappeared
d) the fact that attitudes to the poor have not changed

4 The author talks about the idea that if people do not work it is because they do not
want to. According to the author, this is
a) his own attitude.
b) a characteristically modern attitude.
c) a characteristically Victorian attitude.
d) an attitude that has existed at least since the sixteenth century.

5 According to the passage
a) widows and unmarried mothers are both regarded as 'deserving poor'.
b) widows are regarded as 'deserving poor' but not unmarried mothers.
c) unmarried mothers should be regarded as more deserving than widows.
d) both widows and unmarried mothers are regarded as 'undeserving poor'.

6 'Belied' (line 16) means
a) proved
b) disproved
c) illustrated
d) concealed

7 'The belief' (line 16) is that
a) if healthy people are poor it is because they are lazy.
b) so-called relief institutions are unsatisfactory.
c) the facts of economic life make it impossible for poverty to lead to the workhouse.
d) relief institutions should deter custom.

8 Why did the pioneers of the workhouse want the labouring classes to be afraid of it?
a) in order to punish them
b) to encourage them to find work and accommodation
c) because the parish was a hard taskmaster
d) to deter custom

9 According to the passage, public attitudes to those who do not work
a) are no better now than they used to be.
b) were at their worst in Victorian times.
c) are much better now than before.
d) are still moralistic and unsympathetic.

10 The word 'them', in line 4, refers to
a) the harrowing tales of human need.
b) the attitudes of Victorian days.
c) the workhouse and the poor laws.
d) our policies towards the deprived.

Second passage

Sleep

We all know that the normal human daily cycle of activity is of some 7–8 hours' sleep
alternating with some 16–17 hours' wakefulness and that, broadly speaking, the sleep
normally coincides with the hours of darkness. Our present concern is with how easily
and to what extent this cycle can be modified.

The question is no mere academic one. The ease, for example, with which people can   5
change from working in the day to working at night is a question of growing importance

in industry where automation calls insistently for round-the-clock working of machines. It normally takes from five days to one week for a person to adapt to a reversed routine of sleep and wakefulness, sleeping during the day and working at night. Unfortunately, it is often the case in industry that shifts are changed every week; a person may work from   10 12 midnight to 8 a.m. one week, 8 a.m. to 4 p.m. the next, and 4 p.m. to 12 midnight the third and so on. This means that no sooner has he got used to one routine than he has to change to another, so that much of his time is spent neither working nor sleeping very efficiently.

One answer would seem to be longer periods on each shift, a month, or even three months. Recent research by Bonjer (1960) of the Netherlands, however, has shown   15 that people on such systems will revert to their normal habits of sleep and wakefulness during the week-end and that this is quite enough to destroy any adaptation to night work built up during the week.

The only real solution appears to be to hand over the night shift to a corps of permanent night workers whose nocturnal wakefulness may persist through all week-ends and   20 holidays. An interesting study of the domestic life and health of night-shift workers was carried out by Brown in 1957. She found a high incidence of disturbed sleep, digestive disorder and domestic disruption among those on alternating day and night shifts, but no abnormal occurrence of these symptoms among those on permanent night work.

This latter system then appears to be the best long-term policy, but meanwhile   25 something may be done to relieve the strains of alternate day and night work by selecting those people who can adapt most quickly to the changes of routine. One way of knowing when a person has adapted is by measuring his performance, but this can be laborious. Fortunately, we again have a physiological measure which correlates reasonably well with the behavioural one, in this case performance at various times of the day or night,   30 and which is easier to take. This is the level of body temperature, as taken by an ordinary clinical thermometer. People engaged in normal daytime work will have a high temperature during the hours of wakefulness and a low one at night; when they change to night work the pattern will only gradually reverse to match the new routine and the speed with which it does so parallels, broadly speaking, the adaptation of the body as a whole,   35 particularly in terms of performance and general alertness. Therefore by taking body temperature at intervals of two hours throughout the period of wakefulness it can be seen how quickly a person can adapt to a reversed routine, and this could be used as a basis for selection. So far, however, such a form of selection does not seem to have been applied in practice.   40

From 'Sleep and Dreams' by Robert Wilkinson

Exercise b

Choose the best answer to each question.

1 The main theme of the passage is
a) the effects of lack of sleep.
b) sleep and body temperature.
c) how easily people can get used to working at night.
d) the effect of automation on working efficiency.

2 Why is the question 'no mere academic one'?
a) Because of research by Bonjer and Brown.
b) Because sleep normally coincides with the hours of darkness.
c) Because some people can change their sleeping habits easily.
d) Because shift work in industry requires people to change their sleeping habits.

3 The main problem about night work is that
a) people do not want the inconvenience of working on night shifts.
b) people are disturbed by changing from day to night routines and back.
c) not all industries work at the same hours.
d) it is difficult to find a corps of good night workers.

4 The best answer to the problem seems to be
a) not to change shifts from one week to the next.
b) to have longer periods on each shift.
c) to employ people who will always work at night.
d) to find ways of selecting people who adapt quickly.

5 Scientists are able to measure adaptation by taking body temperature because
a) body temperature is a good basis for selection.
b) people have low temperatures at night.
c) the temperature reverses when the routine is changed.
d) people have high temperatures when they are working efficiently.

6 'The third' (line 12) means
a) the third week
b) the third shift
c) a third of the time
d) the third routine

7 'Another' (line 13) means
a) another routine
b) another shift
c) another week
d) another person

8 'This latter system' (line 25) refers to
a) Brown's research.
b) spending a month or even three months on each shift.
c) having the same people on night shift all the time.
d) alternating day and night shifts.

9 'This' (line 28) refers to
a) a person's performance.
b) measuring a person's performance.
c) the physiological measure.
d) knowing when a person has adapted.

10 'This' (line 31) refers to
a) a physiological measure.
b) performance at various times of the day or night.
c) the level of body temperature.
d) a person's performance.

Teaching unit 4: Understanding complicated sentences 2

In teaching unit 3 we looked at a certain kind of structure which can make sentences difficult to understand. This unit contains examples of some other complicated structures, together with exercises to give you practice in dealing with them.

Conditionals, negatives, etc.

Always pay very careful attention to sentences containing words like 'if', 'supposing', 'assuming', 'provided that', 'unless', or negative words like 'no', 'hardly', etc. These words do not always make as much impression as the nouns, verbs, adjectives etc., especially in long and complicated sentences, so it can be easy to overlook them – but of course they have a very important effect on the meaning.

Exercise a

Read these sentences and answer the questions.

1 *Devaney's policy is one that has always appealed to the great mass of the public, and there is absolutely no doubt that he will become president at the next election (assuming he decides to offer himself as a candidate) with a very large majority.*
   Is it certain that Devaney will be the next president? If not, why not?

2 *He said that he certainly would not pay me the money I asked for unless I categorically refused to see Gromek again.*
   If I see Gromek again, will I get the money?

3 *I do not think anything could possibly be more likely to upset me, all things considered, than the idea of not going mountain-climbing this summer.*
   Do I want to go climbing or not?

4 *If I had realised what he had in mind, I would hardly have let him know that I had not the least intention of going to Essex.*
   Did I tell him I did not want to go to Essex?

5 *Not only does she not enjoy listening to people talking about philosophy, but she is also inclined to get very irritated by any conversation which is not directly connected with herself.*
   Does she prefer conversations about philosophy or about herself?

Inversion

Sometimes in conditional sentences, the word 'if' is left out and a special word-order (inversion – the word-order of questions) is used instead. Look out for sentences which, although they are not questions, begin with 'were', 'should' or 'had'.

Examples:

a) *Were we asked to say what we regard as the purpose of life, most of us would have difficulty in answering.* (= *If we were asked...*)

b) *Had I known earlier, I should have warned you.* (= *If I had known...*)

c) *Should the Conservatives win the next election, there is likely to be a significant change of economic policy.* (= *If the Conservatives win...*)

Note that 'should' is also used (with no real meaning) in some other constructions. This happens, for instance, in sentences that begin 'It is...that...'
Example: *It is interesting that she should want to move to London.* (= *...that she wants...*)
It also happens after 'in case', in past contexts.
Example: *He prepared a careful story in case the tax inspector should call.*

Inversion is also used in sentences that begin with the expressions 'no sooner', 'hardly', 'scarcely', and with some expressions including the word 'only'.

Exercise b

Rewrite these sentences so as to express the same ideas in a more simple way.

1 George insisted that the party would have gone much better had he been invited.
2 Were I given the chance of a year's holiday, I should travel round the world.
3 She explained that no sooner had she closed the door, because of the draught, than a terrible rattling noise was heard and a white light appeared.
4 Only if I trusted you completely could I tell you all my plans.

Double structures

A lot of English structures have two parts (e.g. both... and...; so... that...). When a sentence is long, it is not always easy to keep both parts in your head at the same time.

Exercise c

Read the following pairs of sentences slowly; note how the structure of the first sentence of each pair is repeated in the second.

1a) He was so fat that he could not see his feet.
 b) The plan he put forward was so difficult for his assistants, even the most experienced, to understand and put into action, that there was little chance of its having any material result.
2a) I regard her as one of my best friends.
 b) Luke Parslow was regarded by practically all the people who knew him, including a number who were well qualified to judge such matters, as one of the most promising young lawyers in the county.
3a) The more I learn, the more I forget.
 b) The more often I saw her, in that summer which was remarkable in so many different and exciting ways, and which will remain in my memory long after later summers have faded from my mind, the more I realised how fascinated I was by her exotic, mysterious and intriguing personality.

Practice text

Read the following text slowly and carefully until you are sure that you understand it as well as possible. (There are no questions.) Do not worry if there are one or two words you cannot understand, but pay very great attention to the structure of the sentences, and make sure that you can see clearly how each one is built up.

Dear *Time Out*,
If you in any way make pretence to being the sort of paper that espouses and encourages change then surely you will wish to present to your readers information in such a way as will inspire them to think for themselves and make up their own minds about the events that happen around them. So having the correct information, they will act as individuals   5
in accordance with their conscience in such a way as to promote the kind of change that is rooted not in prejudice but in common sense.
  This you appear to do within your reportage of political and social events most effectively. It's when we come to the arts – and the theatre in particular – that your failings become most apparent. Not only do you not encourage open-mindedness in   10

the potential spectator (surely an essential prerequisite for any understanding or appreciation
of the arts) but you positively try and prevent him reaching his own conclusion about
the work. For one's appreciation and understanding of a play must inevitably be influenced
by what one has read about it previous to arriving at the theatre.

Only if I was a dummy could such a write-up as 'It is not only a massive statement   15
on personal and political corruption, treachery and decay, but an equally forceful statement on the nature of theatre itself. It is visually superb, crisp and austere, without
a wasted moment or movement, and should explode in the smug triteness of London
theatre like a truckload of adrenalin' move me to visit this event. Like the blandest of
advertisements it beats me with its words till I'm senseless, yet tells me about the show   20
absolutely nothing whatsoever.

A reader's letter in *Time Out*

Practice unit 4.1

Read the text slowly and carefully and then answer the questions that follow.

Notes on the great Mozart mystery

Mozart is troubling me again, though I must say that what has given rise to the recurrence
of the trouble this time has been well worth it, being the performance of all the piano
concertos in a series of seven concerts by Barenboim and the English Chamber Orchestra.

Barenboim is himself a prodigy hardly less Protean* than Mozart. One of that group
of younger musicians who are not content simply to play their chosen instrument, but   5
who are always experimenting with musical workshops and the like, he has an extraordinary range of achievements and activities to his credit. He conducted from the
keyboard of course, during the series, but that was comparatively simple (ho ! how's
that 'comparatively' for impudence?); he also, however, conducts opera (*Figaro* at the
Edinburgh Festival this year), and does a lot of chamber-music and television, and   10
I expect he'll start to sing soon.

Anyway, the concerts – three last autumn and the remaining four just completed –
have been enormously refreshing and exhilarating. (There is something especially
rewarding about hearing, in a short period, the entire range of a composer's work in
one particular form; I always used to go to Klemperer's regular cycle of the Beethoven   15
symphonies, and before that, long before you were born, my dear, to Furtwängler's,
but the habit has rather died out now, though Haitink revived it, with huge success –
goodness, I had a splendid time – last year.) But the experience did raise, once again, and
in an acute form, the Mozart Problem.

The Mozart Problem consists, in essence, of the question: how did the music he wrote   20
get into his head in the first place? Obviously, the sources of artistic creation are always
invisible and inexplicable; we can trace influences and see how ideas developed, but we
still cannot say what creation actually *is*. Yet I cannot help feeling that in Mozart's
case there is a gap of an entirely different order from that which separates us from the   24
work of other composers. Wagner, if you will pardon the expression, who was probably
the most stupendously original mind in the entire history of art, presents no problems
of the kind that Mozart does, and Beethoven – certainly until the last quartets – is

* *Protean*: able to change easily and quickly

transparent by comparison. The heart of Beethoven beat in a recognisably human way; that of Wagner in an all too human way; nay, Schubert himself is explicable – the feelings, the sufferings, the love, the fecundity of invention, all are recognisable in him   30
as human qualities. But Mozart?

'The language of a composer', Cardus wrote, 'his harmonies, rhythms, melodies, colours and texture, cannot be separated except by pedantic analysis from the mind and sensibility of the artist who happens to be expressing himself through them'.

But that is precisely the trouble; for as far as I can see, Mozart's can. Mozart makes   35
me begin to see ghosts, or at the very least ouija-boards. If you read Beethoven's letters, you feel that you are at the heart of a tempest, a whirlwind, a furnace; and so you should, because you are. If you read Wagner's you feel that you have been run over by a tank, and that, too, is an appropriate response. But if you read Mozart's – and he was a hugely prolific letter-writer – you have no clue at all to the power that drove him and   40
the music it squeezed out of him in such profusion that death alone could stop it; they reveal nothing – *nothing* – that explains it. Of course it is absurd (though the mistake is frequently made) to seek external causes for particular works of music; but with Mozart it is also absurd, or at any rate useless, to seek for internal ones either. Mozart was an instrument. *But who was playing it?*   45

That is what I mean by the Mozart Problem and the anxiety it causes me. In all art, in all anything, there is nothing like the perfection of Mozart, nothing to compare with the range of feeling he explores, nothing to equal the contrast between the simplicity of the materials and the complexity and effect of his use of them. The piano concertos themselves exhibit these truths at their most intense; he was a greater master of this form than   50
of the symphony itself, and to hear every one of them, in the astounding abundance of genius they provide, played as I have so recently heard them played, is to be brought face to face with a mystery which, if we could solve it, would solve the mystery of life itself.

We can see Mozart, from infant prodigy to unmarked grave. We know what he did, what he wrote, what he felt, whom he loved, where he went, what he died of. We pile   55
up such knowledge as a child does bricks; and then we hear the little tripping rondo tune of the last concerto – with which Barenboim, though he had made no attempt at chronological order otherwise, fittingly concluded the series – and the bricks collapse; all our knowledge is useless to explain a single bar of it. It is almost enough to make me believe in – but I have run out of space, and don't have to say it. Put K.595 on the   60
gramophone and say it for me.

From an article in *The Times* by Bernard Levin

Exercise

Choose the best answer to each question.

1   Why does the writer say that Mozart is troubling him again (line 1)?
a)   Because he has recently been to some Mozart concerts.
b)   Because of Barenboim's interpretation of Mozart.
c)   Because Mozart is a mysterious composer.
d)   Because of the Mozart Problem.

2   The word 'it', in line 2, refers to
a)   what has given rise to the recurrence of the trouble.
b)   the Mozart Problem.
c)   the trouble.
d)   the price of the tickets for Barenboim's concerts.

3 Why does the writer seem to admire Barenboim?
a) Because Barenboim is young.
b) Because he is always experimenting.
c) Because he can do a lot of different things very well.
d) Because he conducts opera.

4 The word 'anyway', in line 12, is closest in meaning to
a) by any means
b) in whatever way they were performed
c) in fact
d) to return to the point

5 The writer found it 'enormously refreshing and exhilarating' (line 13) to be able to hear in a short time
a) all Mozart's piano concertos.
b) all Mozart's works.
c) all the Beethoven symphonies conducted by Klemperer.
d) all the Beethoven symphonies conducted by Barenboim.

6 The words 'my dear', in line 16, are addressed to
a) the editor.
b) the reader.
c) the writer's wife.
d) a particular person the writer is talking to.

7 What was 'the experience' (line 18)?
a) the Mozart Problem
b) hearing the Mozart concertos
c) the splendid time the writer had
d) Haitink's revival of the habit

8 The expression 'a gap of an entirely different order' (line 24) suggests that
a) Mozart's music is easier to appreciate than that of other composers.
b) Mozart arranged his work differently from other composers.
c) the problem of understanding where the composer's inspiration came from is much bigger in Mozart's case.
d) Mozart's music is more difficult to appreciate than that of other composers.

9 Why does the writer say 'Wagner (if you will pardon the expression)' in line 25?
a) To show his respect for Wagner.
b) To apologise for the way in which he refers to Wagner.
c) Because it is an exaggeration to say that Wagner had a stupendously original mind.
d) Because he feels that Wagner's name is something like a dirty word.

10 What is meant by 'Beethoven . . . is transparent by comparison' (lines 27–8)?
a) His music is easier to understand that Wagner's.
b) His music is easier to understand than Mozart's.
c) His sources of inspiration are much clearer than Mozart's.
d) His music is easier to understand than that of all other composers.

11 The word 'them', in line 34, refers to
a) the Mozart piano concertos.
b) a composer's harmonies, rhythms, melodies, colours and texture.
c) pedantic analysis.
d) the mind and sensibility of the artist.

12 'Mozart's can', in line 35, means
a) Mozart's human feelings can be understood.
b) Mozart's music can be understood.
c) Mozart's harmonies, rhythms, etc. can be separated from one another.
d) Mozart's musical language can be separated from his personality.

13 'So you should' (lines 37–8) means
a) You should feel that you are at the heart of a tempest.
b) You should read Beethoven's letters.
c) You should appreciate Beethoven.
d) You would feel the same if you were Beethoven.

14 'Because you are' (line 38). You are what?
a) at the heart of a tempest
b) in existence
c) like Beethoven
d) reading Beethoven's letters

15 The word 'it', in the expression 'explains it', in line 42, means
a) a clue
b) the power that drove Mozart
c) Mozart's music
d) Mozart's life

16 In the expression 'internal ones' (line 44), the word 'ones' refers to
a) people
b) ideas
c) works of music
d) causes

17 The word 'them', in line 49, refers to
a) the feelings he explores
b) the complexity and effect
c) the materials
d) the instruments of the orchestra

18 The word 'their', in line 50, refers to
a) the complexity and effect of his use of them
b) the materials
c) the piano concertos
d) these truths

19 In the expression 'a single bar of it' (line 59), 'it' refers to
a) a tune in the last concerto
b) all Mozart's music
c) the knowledge we pile up
d) the series

20 The 'Mozart Problem', as defined by the author, is that
a) it is difficult to understand Mozart's music.
b) it is difficult to see any connection between Mozart's life and personality and his music.
c) Mozart said nothing about his music in his letters.
d) Mozart's music is different from that of composers like Beethoven or Wagner.

Section B:
Open-ended tests and summary-writing

Teaching unit 5: Open-ended tests

In the multiple choice tests in units 1–4, all you had to do was to understand the text and to choose the best answer from the alternatives which were offered. 'Open-ended' tests are a little more difficult: you not only have to understand the text, but you have to work out for yourself how to express the answer. They test composition as well as comprehension.

Using your own words

It is a good idea, when you answer questions like these, to use your own words as far as possible. Obviously you cannot avoid using some words from the text – if the passage is about pigeons, for instance, it is difficult to write about it without using the word 'pigeon' – but you should be careful not to use long expressions or whole sentences from the passage in your answers.

For example, imagine that a comprehension passage in an exam contains the sentence 'Carruthers' main reason for deciding to rob the Anglo-Patagonian Bank was the severe financial crisis which had recently overtaken his family'. If you were asked 'Why did Carruthers decide to rob a bank?' it would not be a very good idea to write 'Because of the severe financial crisis which had recently overtaken his family'. This might make the reader feel that you had not really understood the text, or that you did not know enough English to express the meaning in a different way. A much better answer would be 'Because his family were now very short of money'.

Complete sentences

Write the answer in its most natural form, as you think an English person would express it. We do not normally say or write 'complete sentences' in answer to questions beginning with words like 'why', 'where' or 'when'.

Example:
Question: Who was suffering from a financial crisis?
Answer: Carruthers' family. (Not Carruthers' family was suffering . . .)
Question: Why did Carruthers decide to rob a bank?
Answer: Because his family . . . (Not Carruthers decided to rob a bank because his family . . .)

Exercise

Read the following text and then answer the questions.

The bohemian* marihuana smoker

There is a very real conflict between the values of the police and those of the bohemian marihuana smoker. For whereas the policeman values upright masculinity, deferred gratification, sobriety and respectability, the bohemian embraces values concerned with overt expressivity in behaviour and clothes, and the pursuit of pleasure unrelated to – and indeed disdaining – work. The bohemian in fact threatens the *reality* of the police-   5
man. He lives without work, he pursues pleasure without deferring gratification, he enters sexual relationships without undergoing the obligations of marriage, he dresses freely in a world where uniformity in clothing is seen as a mark of respectability and reliability.

At this point it is illuminating to consider the study made by R. Blum and associates   10
of American policemen working in the narcotics field. When asked to describe the outstanding personal and social characteristics of the illicit drug-user, the officers most frequently mentioned moral degeneracy, unwillingness to work, insecurity and instability, pleasure orientation, inability to cope with life problems, weakness and inadequate personality. They rated marihuana users as being a greater community menace than   15
the Mafia. The following quote by an intelligent and capable officer is illustrative:

'I tell you there's something about users that bugs me. I don't know what it is exactly. You want me to be frank? OK. Well, I can't stand them; I mean I *really* can't stand them. Why? Because they bother me personally. They're *dirty*, that's what they are, filthy. They make my skin crawl.   20

'It's funny but I don't get that reaction to ordinary criminals. You pinch a burglar or a pickpocket and you understand each other; you know how it is, you stand around yacking, maybe even crack a few jokes. But Jesus, these guys, they're a danger. You know what I mean, they're like Commies or some of those CORE people.

'There are some people you can feel sorry for. You know, you go out and pick up   25
some poor chump of a paper hanger [bad-cheque writer] and he's just a drunk and life's got him all bugged. You can understand a poor guy like that. It's different with anybody who'd use drugs.'

Similarly a British policeman – Detective Inspector Wyatt, formerly head of Essex drugs squad – is quoted as saying about cannabis* users: 'Never in my experience   30
have I met up with such filth and degradation which follows some people who are otherwise quite intelligent. You become a raving bloody idiot so that you can become more lovable.'

Thus the drug-user evokes an immediate gut reaction, while most criminals are immediately understandable in both motives and life style. For the criminal is merely   35
cheating at the rules of a game which the policeman himself plays, whereas the bohemian is sceptical of the validity of the game itself and casts doubts on the world-view of both policemen and criminal.

It is not sufficient to argue that the marihuana smoker is on paper a member of a group with which the police are likely to conflict. Two intervening variables determine   40
whether such a conflict will actually take place: the visibility and the vulnerability of the group. The drug-taker, because of his long hair and – to the police – bizarre dress, is an exceedingly visible target for police action. The white middle-class dropout creates for himself the stigmata out of which prejudice can be built, he voluntarily places himself in the position in which the Negro unwittingly finds himself. Moreover, he moves to   45

* *bohemian*: living outside the normal rules and conventions of society
  cannabis: marihuana

areas such as Notting Hill where he is particularly vulnerable to apprehension and arrest, unlike the middle-class neighbourhoods he comes from where he was to some extent protected by 'good' family and low police vigilance.

From 'The bohemian marihuana smoker' by Jock Young

1   What is the difference, according to the passage, between the marihuana smoker's attitude to dress and that of the police?
2   What is the difference in their attitudes to work?
3   What is meant by saying that the bohemian 'threatens the reality 'of the policeman?
4   Who are 'they' in line 15?
5   In what way did these people think that drug users were worse than the Mafia?
6   Who are 'they' and 'them' in lines 18–19?
7   What is meant by 'it's funny' in line 21?
8   Who is 'you' in lines 21 and 22?
9   Who is 'you' in line 32?
10   What is meant by 'on paper' in line 39?
11   Why is the 'visibility of the group' a special reason for conflict with the police?
12   Does the writer feel that marihuana smokers dress in a strange way?
13   In what way are Negroes similar to drug-users?
14   Why is Notting Hill apparently a more dangerous place for a marihuana-smoker to live than the area he comes from?
15   In what way are drug-users seen by the police as a special class of criminal?

Practice unit 5.1

Read the text slowly and carefully, and then answer the questions that follow.

Washoe

A very intensive attempt to teach a chimpanzee to talk was made some years ago by a married couple, both scientists, K. J. and Cathy Hayes. They adopted a baby chimp called Viki, and brought her up in their house exactly as if she were a human child, but using in addition the most sophisticated methods of teaching available. The result was disappointing. After six years of great effort and ingenuity, Viki had learned to utter   5
only four sounds resembling English words. From this and other studies, it looked as if chimpanzees cannot be taught a human language.

So matters stood until June 1966, when another scientist couple, R. A. and Beatrice T. Gardner, began work at the University of Nevada with a female chimpanzee between eight and fourteen months old, whom they named Washoe after the county where the   10
University is situated. Benefiting from the Hayes' experience, the Gardners had had an imaginative new idea. We have seen that most monkeys rely more on visual than on vocal signals. Even the actual vocal apparatus of chimpanzees is very different from man's. So instead of trying to teach *spoken* English, the Gardners decided to teach Washoe American Sign Language, as used by the deaf in North America, in which English words   15
or concepts are represented by signs made with the hands; some of these symbols are representational, others are arbitrary, and all can be combined according to principles of English grammar and syntax. The Gardners and their colleagues brought up Washoe

in shifts so that she never lacked for affectionate human company. They played all sorts
of games with her and seem to have given her a very good time. All the time they   20
were chattering among themselves in Sign Language, for it is known that simply being
exposed to adults talking helps human children to learn to talk. They encouraged Washoe
to imitate them, prompted her to get a sign right by repeating it themselves or by placing
her hands in the right position, introduced plenty of toys and other objects to increase her
vocabulary, encouraged her to 'babble' with her hands, as a child does with his voice,   25
and rewarded her for correct usage by tickling her, which she greatly enjoyed.

The results of all this were as follows. After twenty-two months of teaching, Washoe
could use thirty-four words correctly in the appropriate circumstances. (She was only
counted as knowing a word if three observers independently saw her use it correctly and
without prompting.) Whenever Washoe learned a new word, she very soon and quite   30
spontaneously transferred it from a particular object, such as the key of a cupboard, to
a whole class of objects, such as all keys. She would spontaneously call the humans'
attention to objects by making the correct signs. She used the sign for 'dog' when she
saw a picture of a dog or even heard a dog bark without seeing it; evidently, like the
dolphins, she had the capacity, previously supposed to be unique to man, of transposing   35
patterns from one sense to another.

All this is remarkable, but Washoe did more. Without any prompting and apparently
quite spontaneously, as soon as she had about ten signs in her repertoire, Washoe began to
invent combinations of signs and use them in a perfectly appropriate way. Among combinations which she invented are: *open food drink*, for opening the refrigerator; *go sweet*,   40
for being carried to a raspberry bush; *open flower*, to be let through the gate to a flower
garden; and *listen eat*, at the sound of an alarm clock signalling meal-time. Just before the
Gardners published their first results (in August 1969), Washoe had learned the pronouns
I–me and *you*, 'so that combinations that resemble short sentences have begun to appear'.
It only remains to add that Washoe's learning was accelerating – she had learned 4 signs   45
in the first seven months, 9 in the next, and 21 in the last seven months.

Since Washoe unmistakably combines and recombines signs to describe objects and
situations new to her in perfectly appropriate ways, this wonderful experiment seems to
have established beyond doubt that a chimpanzee is capable of learning true language.
True, at three years of age, she only has thirty-four words; at the equivalent age in   50
terms of development, namely five years old, the average human child has a vocabulary
of hundreds of words and makes sentences averaging 4·6 words in length. Sheer
numerical differences of this kind may be important for the potentialities of human
language. But the Gardners' achievement remains epoch-making. An animal has been
taught to use true language, to communicate with human teachers.   55

From 'Language and Animal Signals' by Claire and W. R. S. Russell

Exercise

1   What was the main difference between the results of the two experiments with Viki
    and Washoe?
2   What was the main reason for this difference?
3   What is meant by the expression 'so matters stood' (line 8)?
4   Why did the Gardners decide to use sign language instead of spoken English in their
    experiment?
5   What does the word 'all' refer to, in line 17?

6   How did the experimenters manage to ensure that Washoe always had company?

7   What does 'they' refer to, in line 20?

8   Why did the experimenters talk among themselves in sign language?

9   What is meant by 'in the appropriate circumstances' (line 28)?

10 What was the point of the rule about three observers?

11 Does the text suggest that there are other animals besides chimpanzees that can use language in a way similar to humans?

12 'In a perfectly appropriate way' (line 39) means...

13 'All this is remarkable, but Washoe did more' (line 37). What exactly was the more remarkable thing that she did?

14 What was the main difference between Washoe's use of language and that of a human child at the same stage?

15 The three-year-old Washoe is compared, not with a child of the same age, but with a five-year-old. Why is this?

16 How long, roughly, had the experiment lasted at the time when this report was written?

Practice unit 5.2

Read the text carefully and then answer the questions that follow.

I love my lawyer

Folsom Prison, October 9, 1965

I'm perfectly aware that I'm in prison, that I'm a Negro, that I've been a rapist, and that I have a Higher Uneducation. I never know what significance I'm supposed to attach to these factors. But I have a suspicion that, because of these aspects of my character, 'free–normal–educated' people rather expect me to be more reserved, penitent, remorse-   5
ful, and not too quick to shoot off my mouth on certain subjects. But I let them down, disappoint them, make them gape at me in a sort of stupor, as if they're thinking: 'You've got your nerve! Don't you realize that you owe a debt to society?' My answer to all such thoughts lurking in their split-level heads, crouching behind their squinting bombardier eyes, is that the blood of Vietnamese peasants has paid off all my debts;   10
that the Vietnamese people, afflicted with a rampant disease called Yankees, through their sufferings – as opposed to the 'frustration' of fat-assed American geeks safe at home worrying over whether to have bacon, ham, or sausage with their grade-A eggs in the morning, while Vietnamese worry each morning whether the Yankees will gas them, burn them up, or blow away their humble pads★ in a hail of bombs – have canceled   15
all my IOUs.

But what matters is that I have fallen in love with my lawyer! Is that surprising? A convict is expected to have a high regard for *anyone* who comes to his aid, who tries to help him and who expends time, energy, and money in an effort to set him free. But can a convict really love a lawyer? It goes against the grain. Convicts hate lawyers. To   20
walk around a prison yard and speak well of a lawyer is to raise the downcast eyebrows of felons who've been bitten by members of the Bar and Grill★. Convicts are convinced that lawyers must have a secret little black book which no one else is ever allowed to see,

★ *pads*: homes (slang)
  The Bar and Grill: a lawyers' association

a book that schools lawyers in an esoteric morality in which the Highest Good is
treachery, and crossing one's dumb and trusting client the noblest of deeds. It was   25
learned by the convicts that I'd gotten busted with some magazines given to me by my
lawyer and that I was thrown in the Hole for it. Convicts smiled knowingly and told me
that I had gone for the greasy pig, that my lawyer had set me up, and that if I couldn't
see through the plot I was so stupid that I would buy not only the Golden Gate Bridge
but some fried ice cream.   30

It was my turn to smile knowingly. A convict's paranoia is as thick as the prison wall
and just as necessary. Why should we have faith in anyone? Even our wives and lovers
whose beds we have shared, with whom we have shared the tenderest moments and most
delicate relations, leave us after a while, put us down, cut us clean aloose and treat us like
they hate us, won't even write us a letter, send us a Christmas card every other year,   35
or a quarter for a pack of cigarettes or a tube of toothpaste now and then. All society
shows the convict its ass and expects him to kiss it: the convict feels like kicking it or
putting a bullet in it. A convict sees man's fangs and claws and learns quickly to bare
and unsheath his own, for real and final. To maintain a hold on the ideals and sentiments
of civilization in such circumstances is probably impossible. How much more incredible   40
is it, then, while rooted in this pit, to fall in love, and with a lawyer! Use a lawyer, yes:
use anybody. Even tell the lawyer that you're in love. But you will always know when
you are lying and even if you could manage to fool the lawyer you could never manage
to fool yourself.

And why does it make you sad to see how everything hangs by such thin and whimsical   45
threads? Because you're a dreamer, an incredible dreamer, with a tiny spark hidden
somewhere inside you which cannot die, which even you cannot kill or quench and
which tortures you horribly because all the odds are against its continual burning. In the
midst of the foulest decay and putrid savagery, this spark speaks to you of beauty, of
human warmth and kindness, of goodness, of greatness, of heroism, of martyrdom, and   50
it speaks to you of love.

I suppose that I should be honest and, before going any further, admit that my lawyer
is a woman – or maybe I should have held back with that piece of the puzzle - a very
excellent, unusual, and beautiful woman. I know that *she* believes that I do not really
love her and that I am confusing a combination of lust and gratitude for love. Lust and   55
gratitude I feel abundantly, but I also love this woman. And I fear that, believing that I
do not love her, she will act according to that belief.

From *Soul on Ice* by Eldridge Cleaver

Exercise

1 Why, according to Cleaver, do 'free–normal–educated' people expect him not to give
   his opinions?
2 What do you think he means by a 'Higher Uneducation' (line 3)?
3 How does he let people down and disappoint them?
4 Why does he think he's got as much right to talk as other people?
5 What does he mean by saying 'The blood of Vietnamese peasants has paid off all my
   debts'?
6 'Their', in line 12, refers to...
7 Why is it surprising that a convict should fall in love with his lawyer?
8 What was he 'thrown in the Hole' for?
9 What did the other convicts think of his lawyer's giving him magazines?

10 What do you think is meant by 'my lawyer had set me up'?

11 What kind of a person would buy 'not only the Golden Gate Bridge but some fried ice cream'?

12 Why do convicts need to be suspicious of other people?

13 What are 'such circumstances' (line 40)?

14 What is 'this pit' (line 41)?

15 Who is 'you' in lines 42–3?

16 What do convicts think is a lawyer's attitude to criminals?

17 How do they think lawyers should be treated?

Practice unit 5.3

Read the following text slowly and carefully and then answer the questions.

Education: a father's experience

Mr Lucas is a bus driver who left school at fourteen; a man in whom large areas of curiosity, delight and intelligence had lain dormant until his daughter passed the scholarship exam. To hear him speak now is to hear him use words like 'culture' and 'civilization', if not with full confidence at least with a very real sense of what their meanings reside in. 5

'Now when your child is coming along and going to grammar school, you begin to get excited, you begin to be interested, and you want to know more things. That's how it was with us. It was a wonderful thing for us our children learning all these new things. Now when I was at school we learned history and geography and it was all battles and such like. But for our Mary history and geography aren't all like that, they're bigger 10 things. It's as if she can see ten times, a hundred times, as much as we were taught. She doesn't talk about *battles*. Now we went out on a coach trip up in the Yorkshire Dales and she goes poking in the fields and she hoicks out of a field this here thing. Come and have a look out in our garden. Dost tha' see it? Now that's a fossilized fern is that, and you know I'd have kicked a dozen of them things over and I wouldn't have known what it was. Aye, she explained all this and how it happened thousands and thousands of years 16 before all these battles were thought on!

'Na, then, I've been 35 years with the Bus Company and you get to be having privileges after all that time – like free travel. Now we never used that, but when the children got to school we started having this free travel. Coach trips all over the place. We 20 went to Sherwood Forest – now that's a funny place – have you ever noticed what it's like yourself when you go through it?...No, you haven't. I didn't think you would have done. Next time you go through Sherwood Forest, just you stop that car of yours and get out and get a hand full of soil and have a look at it, and you'll find it's all pebbles and sand as if it was on the beach. And that's just what it was – a beach! Our 25 Mary told us all about that. She explained it all to us, and it was wonderful. One time I saw rocks, they were just rocks and stones, and I'd kick them over and never think about them. But now I look at them, and I wonder whether that's volcanic or a bit of glacier or a fossil, and it's exciting knowing them things.

'And it's not only rocks either. It's cathedrals and things like that. When you go round with her she talks about the architecture and you listen to it. And you'll even go and 31 put sixpence in that little box at the end of the church and buy one of these little books and read up all the history of it all. Now at one time, I'd never have done that. Aye, aye,

aye, there's lots of things like that and you get very excited about them. Now, when our Mary went to college, it was down in London and you mightn't have heard about this,   35 but there's one of these here big music composers and he's called Benjamin Britten. Well, this here chap, Benjamin Britten, he writes these big operas. Na then, when he had his first go at this, the Queen comes and watches it, and he doesn't want it to be a flop and a farce does he? So he goes to one of these colleges and all the students work it out for him. They sing and dance it on the stage. Now they had a go at these operas of his   40 before the Queen saw them, at this college where our Mary was. Now you wouldn't find out things like that if you hadn't had children who went to school, would you? There's this here Royal Festival Hall in London that's one of the best places in the world for this here music, and as I say it's only since our Mary's been going to school and college that I've ever thought about this. Last summer the wife and I went on a trip to   45 London. We went to the British Museum. Now at one time that's the *last* place we'd have gone to, but I was filled with wonderment in that British Museum. We went into one big room where it was all about the civilization of Babylon, and there were these great big statues that they'd fetched all the way back from Babylon. My! you should go and see them! Great big things they were, made them to last in them days, didn't they?   50 Aye, and all that civilization gone – you get to thinking about that. All their civilization has gone but ours is here. Now how does all that come about?...Education brings all kinds of things, doesn't it? – same as the people round here, they just think you go to school and then you go to work, but it's not like that when you've been educated. You can see big things like a civilization, you don't think about the job you're going to   55 do.'

From an interview quoted in *Education and the Working Class* by Brian Jackson and Dennis Marsden

Exercise

1 Who are 'us' in line 8?
2 Why does Mary not talk about battles?
3 Why has Mr Lucas put a fossilised fern in his garden?
4 Why does he get free travel on buses?
5 When did he start taking advantage of this?
6 What is meant by saying that Sherwood Forest 'was a beach'?
7 What does 'it', in line 26, refer to?
8 What are 'them things' (line 29)?
9 What is the meaning of 'it all' (line 33)?
10 'This' (line 35) refers to...
11 What did Benjamin Britten do in order to make sure of a good performance for the Queen?
12 What is meant by 'he had his first go at this' (lines 37–8)?
13 What is 'this' in line 45?
14 Who are 'they' in line 49?
15 What is meant by 'made them to last' (line 50)?
16 What does Mr Lucas mean when he says 'You get to thinking about that' (line 51)
17 What was the general effect on Mr Lucas of his daughter's education?
18 Can you mention several of his new interests?

Teaching unit 6: Introduction to summary

In comprehension tests and examinations, you are often asked to summarise a passage – to give the main points in a short paragraph of perhaps 100 words. This is particularly difficult to do when the passage is written in a complicated way, with long sentences or a lot of unusual vocabulary. You need to 'see through' the words to the idea (often a very simple one) which is behind them. The following exercises will give you practice in doing this.

Exercise a

Each of these sentences can be rewritten much more briefly without really changing the meaning. Read them carefully, and then rewrite them in as few words as possible (between two and ten).

1 I am telling no more than the truth when I say that George is a habitual consumer of tobacco.
2 In her employment, Mary showed a thoroughly satisfactory degree of energy and efficiency.
3 My sister shows a distinct tendency to prefer the company of people who are no longer in the first flower of youth.
4 It is undeniable that the large majority of non-native learners of English experience a number of problems in attempting to master the phonetic patterns of the language.
5 I have been obliged to abandon the belief, which I previously held, in the existence of a benevolent white-haired bearded figure who was accustomed to visit private houses on the anniversary of the birth of the founder of the Christian religion, in order to distribute gifts to young people.
6 Tea, whether of the China or Indian variety, is well known to be high on the list of those beverages which are most frequently drunk by the inhabitants of the British Isles.
7 It is not uncommon to encounter sentences which, though they contain a great number of words and are constructed in a highly complex way, none the less turn out on inspection to convey very little meaning of any kind.
8 One of the most noticeable phenomena in any big city, such as London or Paris, is the steadily increasing number of petrol-driven vehicles, some in private ownership, others belonging to the public transport system, which congest the roads and render rapid movement more difficult year by year.
9 'The main problem with which I am faced is to decide whether it is preferable to continue in existence, or whether it would, on balance, be a more advisable policy to abandon the struggle.' (Shakespeare)

Exercise b

Read the text carefully and answer the question that follows.

Adolescent students

In dealing with students on the high-school level – that is, the second, third, and fourth year of high school – we must bear in mind that to some degree they are at a difficult psychological stage, generally called adolescence. Students at this level are likely to be confused mentally, to be subject to involuntary distractions and romantic dreaminess. They

are basically timid or self-conscious, they lack frankness and are usually very sensitive   5
but hate to admit it. They are motivated either by great ambition, probably out of all
proportion to their capabilities, or by extreme laziness caused by the fear of not succeeding
or attaining their objectives. Fundamentally they want to be kept busy but they refuse
to admit it. They are frequently the victims of earlier poor training, and this makes
every effort doubly hard. They are usually willing to work, but they hate to work   10
without obtaining the results they think they should obtain. Their critical faculties are
beginning to develop and they are critical of their instructors and of the materials they
are given to learn. They are beginning to feel the pressure of time; and although they
seldom say so, they really want to be consulted and given an opportunity to direct their
own affairs, but they need considerable guidance. They seldom admit that they need   15
this guidance and they frequently rebel against it, but if it is intelligently offered they
accept it with enthusiasm. If they are healthy they are capable of long periods of con-
centration and an extraordinary amount of work. They are trying, most of them, to form
political ideas and they have a tendency to be either extremely idealistic (which is usually
another term for radical) or conservative, blindly accepting what their fathers and   20
grandfathers believed in. It is in this period that students can be most easily and
permanently influenced. It is the period in which they form strong attachments for their
teachers. Their outlook on life is usually extremely exaggerated. They are either far too
modest and retiring, or extravagantly boastful. They are much more susceptible to the
influence of a strong personality than to that of a great intelligence. Of all periods of life,   25
this is what may best be called the 'plastic age'.

From *A Language Teacher's Guide* by E. A. Méras

The writer's view of adolescents can be summed up by saying:
a) They have difficulty in concentrating.
b) Their relationships with adults are difficult.
c) They have a variety of problems and often behave in contradictory ways.
d) Their intelligence is developing.

Exercise c

Read the text carefully, then follow the instructions below.

Violence

Now, if you want to stop violence, if you want to stop wars, how much vitality, how
much of yourself, do you give to it? Isn't it important to you that your children are
killed, that your sons go into the army where they are bullied and butchered? Don't you
care? My God, if that doesn't interest you, what does? Guarding your money? Having
a good time? Taking drugs? Don't you see that this violence in yourself is destroying   5
your children? Or do you see it only as some abstraction?

All right then, if you are interested, attend with all your heart and mind to find out.
Don't just sit back and say, 'Well, tell us all about it'. I point out to you that you cannot
look at anger nor at violence with eyes that condemn or justify and that if this violence is
not a burning problem to you, you cannot put those two things away. So first you have   10
to learn; you have to learn how to look at anger, how to look at your husband, your wife,
your children; you have to listen to the politician, you have to learn why you are not
objective, why you condemn or justify. You have to learn that you condemn and justify
because it is part of the social structure you live in, your conditioning as a German or an Indian

or a Negro or an American or whatever you happen to have been born, with all the   15
dulling of the mind that this conditioning results in. To learn, to discover, something
fundamental you must have the capacity to go deeply. If you have a blunt instrument, a
dull instrument, you cannot go deeply. So what we are doing is sharpening the instrument,
which is the mind – the mind which has been made dull by all this justifying and con-
demning. You can penetrate deeply only if your mind is as sharp as a needle and as   20
strong as a diamond.

It is no good just sitting back and asking, 'How am I to get such a mind'? You have
to want it as you want your next meal, and to have it you must see that what makes your
mind dull and stupid is this sense of invulnerability which has built walls round itself and
which is part of this condemnation and justification. If the mind can be rid of that,   25
then you can look, study, penetrate, and perhaps come to a state that is totally aware of
the whole problem.

To investigate the fact of your own anger you must pass no judgement on it, for the
moment you conceive of its opposite you condemn it and therefore you cannot see it as
it is. When you say you dislike or hate someone that is a fact, although it sounds   30
terrible. If you look at it, go into it completely, it ceases, but if you say, 'I must not hate;
I must have love in my heart', then you are living in a hypocritical world with double
standards. To live completely, fully, in the moment is to live with what is, the actual,
without any sense of condemnation or justification – then you understand it so totally
that you are finished with it. When you see clearly the problem is solved.   35

But can you see the face of violence clearly – the face of violence not only outside you
but inside you, which means that you are totally free from violence because you have
not admitted ideology through which to get rid of it? This requires very deep medita-
tion, not just a verbal agreement or disagreement.

You have now read a series of statements but have you really understood? Your con-   40
ditioned mind, your way of life, the whole structure of the society in which you live,
prevent you from looking at a fact and being entirely free from it *immediately*. You
say, 'I will think about it; I will consider whether it is possible to be free from violence
or not. I will try to be free.' That is one of the most dreadful statements you can make,
'I will try'. There is no trying, no doing your best. Either you do it or you don't do it.   45
You are admitting time while the house is burning. The house is burning as a result of the
violence throughout the world and in yourself and you say, 'Let me think about it.
Which ideology is best to put out the fire?' When the house is on fire, do you argue
about the colour of the hair of the man who brings the water?

From *Freedom from the Known* by J. Krishnamurti

Sum up in one sentence the writer's advice to people who want to stop violence.

Exercise d

Read the text carefully and answer the questions that follow.

The Clark-Trimble experiments

A convenient point of departure is provided by the famous Clark-Trimble experiments
of 1935. Clark-Trimble was not primarily a physicist, and his great discovery of the
Graduated Hostility of Things was made almost accidentally. During some research
into the relation between periods of the day and human bad temper, Clark-Trimble,

a leading Cambridge psychologist, came to the conclusion that low human dynamics in   5
the early morning could not sufficiently explain the apparent hostility of Things at the
breakfast table – the way honey gets between the fingers, the unfoldability of newspapers, etc. In the experiments which finally confirmed him in this view, and which he
demonstrated before the Royal Society in London, Clark-Trimble arranged four
hundred pieces of carpet in ascending degrees of quality, from coarse matting to   10
priceless Chinese silk. Pieces of toast and marmalade, graded, weighed, and measured,
were then dropped on each piece of carpet, and the marmalade-downwards incidence
was statistically analysed. The toast fell right-side-up every time on the cheap carpet,
except when the cheap carpet was screened from the rest (in which case the toast didn't
know that Clark-Trimble had other and better carpets), and it fell marmalade-   15
downwards every time on the Chinese silk. Most remarkable of all, the marmalade-
downwards incidence for the intermediate grades was found to vary *exactly* with the
quality of carpet.

    The success of these experiments naturally switched Clark-Trimble's attention to further
research on *resistentia*, a fact which was directly responsible for the tragic and sudden end   20
to his career when he trod on a garden rake at the Cambridge School of Agronomy.
In the meantime, Noys and Crangenbacker had been doing some notable work in
America. Noys carried out literally thousands of experiments, in which subjects of all
ages and sexes, sitting in chairs of every conceivable kind, dropped various kinds of
pencils. In only three cases did the pencil come to rest within easy reach. Crangen-   25
backer's work in the social-industrial field, on the relation of human willpower to specific
problems such as whether a train or subway will stop with the door opposite you on a
crowded platform, or whether there will be a mail box anywhere on your side of the
street, was attracting much attention.

From 'Report on Resistentialism' by Paul Jennings

1   In a short sentence, say what was proved (according to the writer) by the Clark-Trimble
    experiments.
2   What do you think is the writer's purpose in describing these experiments?

Exercise e

Read the text carefully, then follow the instruction below.

Gun control

A student of the gun control issue will readily perceive the arena is indeed a broad one,
in which we must struggle to preserve the right to keep and bear arms. It is a struggle
which will test whatever there might be of genius in any of us and it is one which will
merit the devoted efforts of every citizen who in the broadest sense can perceive the
relationships which our Bill of Rights liberties bear one to another.   5
    I suggest we begin our affirmative role immediately in the area of crime control. The
truth is that gun control does not equate with crime control. We have an advantage in
this fact which we have neither exploited nor advanced convincingly. It is demonstrable
that in those sections of the country where gun possession is most prevalent, crime is least.
    Encouragingly, many moderate and reasonable men among our opponents are   10
beginning to see that our problem is crime control and that gun control is not going to
have much, if any, effect upon it. Of course, for reasons of their own, some of them still say
gun control is desirable. For these people we can only wonder, as would any good citizen,

what it is they have in mind for us that our possession of guns makes them so nervous.

As long as we concur that any measure of gun control equates with some measure of   15
crime control we are in agreement with those who would eliminate our rights. We would
then again be backed into our defensive position, held for forty years, always losing
a little here and a little there until finally nothing would be left us.

No group of good citizens has ever struggled more conscientiously along the
narrow pathway, between hope and moderation on one hand, and the cold facts of efforts
to abolish our rights on the other, than the leaders of the National Rifle Association.   21
Every gun owner in America should applaud the action taken by the Executive Committee of the NRA in Washington, D.C. on July 12, 1974: '...the NRA opposes any
proposed legislation, at any level of government, which is directed against the
inanimate firearm rather than against the criminal misuse of firearms.'   25

A reasonable degree of order in society must prevail first. Criminals must be controlled first. We are the decent people. We try to be reasonable and we are not fools
even though we have so often made mistakes in the past 40 years.

Many people turn to England as an example for crime control. The fact is that in
England, for hundreds of years, a man found guilty of any one of a number of crimes was
promptly hanged. Now that a more humanistic generation of Englishmen has lately   31
abolished these stern but effective methods, crime – including armed crime – is sky-
rocketing. Recently armed Englishmen, amid a hail of their own bullets, attempted to
kidnap the eldest daughter of the reigning Queen of England! Unbelievable!

From an article in *Guns and Ammo* by Harlan Carter

Try to sum up (in one sentence if possible) the two or three main points which the writer
is making.

Practice unit 6.1

Read the text carefully, and then answer the questions that follow.

Freedom and selfishness

It is always the problem of how to change an ideal into reality that gets in the way of both
the leaders and the people. A thought is not a deed and never will be.

We are not magic men. We cannot imagine something into existence – especially
a change of behavior. Just as we have been conditioned to be what we are now – greedy,
competitive, stingy, mean – so we need to learn to love, to learn to be free.   5

Freedom is a difficult thing to handle. How many people given the complete freedom
to do whatever they like would die of boredom? No structure, no rules, no compulsion
to work from nine to five, no one telling us when to do this, do that – it sounds great
until we try it. We've learned to be directed by so many others – by mommy, daddy,
teacher, principal, boss, policeman, politician, bureaucrat, etc. – that freedom from   10
all this could be overwhelming. Imagine: balling*, eating, sleeping, playing...and...ho,
hum, now what? Where do you go and what do you do when the trip ends?

Give people freedom and they'll do all the things they thought they never had a chance

* *balling*: making love (slang)

to do. But that won't take very long. And after that? After that, my friend, it'll be time
to make your life meaningful.   15

Can you do it if you're free? Can you do it if others no longer require you to do what
they say is best? Authority is only necessary for those who need it. Most of us need it
because we've been taught to believe that we have to be concerned about others. For
instance: 'You're selfish if you think of yourself,' or even: 'Ask not what your country
can do for you, ask what you can do for your country.'   20

Sorry friends, but that's all Christian, authoritarian, manipulative bullshit.* You've
got to get in touch with what your real needs are before you can begin to be of value
to others. The other-directedness of Americans that is promoted by mom, God, and the
flag has pushed us to the precipice of Fascism in this country. We are no longer able to
think for ourselves, we think for the 'good' of others. 'Who am I?' 'What do I really   25
want out of life?' These are considered selfish questions. So a whole society goes down
the drain. So it is with communes, whose members are too eager to help their curious
'brothers,' who find it remarkably easy to create all kinds of physical and figurative mess
and then leave it for the members to clean up.

Challenges to this traditional, other-directed, do-gooder mystique are met with   30
admonitions and scoldings: 'Why are you so selfish, all the time thinking only about
yourself? Don't you have any regard for the rights of others?' (The intent and frequent
effect of such a question is to make one feel guilty and consequently willing to conform
to the 'altruistic'* wishes of others.) And because we have become so confused about
what is really important to us as individuals, we believe these admonitions – and with   35
good reason. Our demands are indeed 'selfish'. As we are no longer capable of knowing
who we really are, we are compelled and desire to be like someone (everyone) else. We
feel we must have money, a new car, power, position, prestige, and an all too material
sense of personal worth.

From *Communes USA* by Richard Fairfield

Exercise

1 Say, in one or two short sentences, what the writer thinks about 'selfishness'.
2 What does he mean by saying 'We are not magic men'?
3 What is the problem about having complete freedom?
4 What does the writer think is the reason for the problem?
5 'It', in line 8, means...
6 What is meant by 'all this', in line 11?
7 Explain the meaning of 'When the trip ends' (line 12)?
8 What does the word 'that' refer to, in line 14?
9 What does 'it' refer to, in line 16?
10 What does 'it' refer to, in line 17?
11 What is the writer's attitude to Christianity?
12 What is the meaning of 'that' in line 21?
13 What does the writer mean by 'other-directedness'?
14 What does he mean by saying that America has been pushed 'to the precipice of Fascism'?
15 Why is the word 'good' in line 25 printed in quotation marks in the passage?
16 What sort of questions 'make one feel guilty', according to the writer?
17 Why, in the writer's view, do people seek personal possessions?

* *bullshit*: nonsense (slang)
  altruistic: unselfish

Practice unit 6.2

Read each text slowly and carefully, and then answer the questions.

First passage

Teaching speech

At the roots of much of our cultural thinking is our actual experience of speech. In Britain the question of good speech is deeply confused, and is in itself a major source of many of the divisions in our culture. It is inevitable, in modern society, that our regional speech-forms should move closer to each other, and that many extreme forms should disappear. But this should be a natural process, as people move and travel and meet more freely,   5 and as they hear different speakers in films, television, and broadcasting. The mistake is to assume that there is already a 'correct' form of modern English speech, which can serve as a standard to condemn all others. In fact 'public-school English', in the form in which many have tried to fix it, cannot now become a common speech-form in the country as a whole: both because of the social distinctions now associated with   10 its use, and because of the powerful influence of American speech-forms. Yet many good forms of modified regional speech are in practice emerging and extending. The barriers imposed by dialect are reduced, in these forms, without the artificiality of imitating a form remote from most people's natural speaking. This is the path of growth. Yet in much speech training, in schools, we go on assuming that there is already one 'correct'   15 form over the country as a whole. Thousands of us are made to listen to our natural speaking with the implication from the beginning that it is *wrong*. This sets up such deep tensions, such active feelings of shame and resentment, that it should be no surprise that we cannot discuss culture in Britain without at once encountering tensions and prejudices deriving from this situation. If we experience speech training as an aspect of our social   20 inferiority, a fundamental cultural division gets built in, very near the powerful emotions of self-respect, family affection, and local loyalty. This does not mean that we should stop speech training. But we shall not get near a common culture in Britain unless we make it a real social process – listening to ourselves and to others with no prior assumption of correctness – rather than the process of imitating a social class which is remote from most   25 of us, leaving us stranded at the end with the 'two-language' problem. Nothing is more urgent than to get rid of this arbitrary association between general excellence and the habits of a limited social group. It is not only that there is much that is good elsewhere. It is also that, if you associate the idea of quality with the idea of class, you may find both rejected as people increasingly refuse to feel inferior on arbitrary social grounds.   30

From *Communications* by Raymond Williams

Exercise a

1 Say clearly and simply what you think is meant by 'our actual experience of speech' (line 1).
2 Explain 'In Britain the question of good speech is deeply confused' (lines 1–2).
3 What is the effect of American speech forms referred to in the passage?
4 What is the writer referring to when he talks about 'a form remote from most people's natural speaking' (line 14)?
5 What is 'this situation' (line 20)?

6   What does 'it', in line 24, refer to?
7   Which is the social class which is 'remote from most of us' (lines 25–6)?
8   What do you think the writer means by the 'two-language problem' (line 26)?
9   Where is 'elsewhere' (line 28)?
10 Does the writer suggest that one English accent is better than others?
11 What is the kind of speech-training that he thinks is wrong?
12 What does he think are the personal and social effects of this kind of speech-training?

Second passage

Received pronunciation

Most of us have an image of such a normal or standard English in pronunciation, and very commonly in Great Britain this is 'Received Pronunciation', often associated with the public schools, Oxford, and the BBC. Indeed, a pronunciation within this range has great prestige throughout the world, and for English taught as a foreign language it is more usually the ideal than any other pronunciation. At the same time, it must be   5
remembered that, so far as the English-speaking countries are concerned, this 'Received Pronunciation' approaches the status of a 'standard' almost only in England: educated Scots, Irishmen, Americans, Australians, and others have their own, different images of a standard form of English.

Even in England it is difficult to speak of a standard in pronunciation. For one thing,   10
pronunciation is infinitely variable, so that even given the will to adopt a single pronunciation, it would be difficult to achieve. The word *dance* may be pronounced in a dozen ways even by people who do not think of themselves as dialect speakers: there is no sure way of any two people saying the same word with precisely the same sound. In this respect, pronunciation much more closely resembles handwriting than spelling.   15
In spelling, there are absolute distinctions which can be learnt and imitated with complete precision: one can know at once whether a word is spelt in a 'standard' way or not. But two persons' handwriting and pronunciation may both be perfectly intelligible, yet have obvious differences without our being able to say which is 'better' or more 'standard'.   20

Moreover, while the easy and quick communications of modern times have mixed up and levelled dialectal distinctions to a great extent, and encouraged the spread of 'neutral', 'normal' pronunciation, the accompanying sociological changes have reduced the prestige of Received Pronunciation. When Mr Robert Graves returned to Oxford in October 1961 to take up the Professorship of Poetry, *The Times* reported him as   25
saying, 'Only the ordinary accent of the undergraduate has changed. In my day you very seldom heard anything but Oxford English; now there is a lot of north country and so on. In 1920 it was prophesied that the Oxford accent would overcome all others. But the regional speech proved stronger. A good thing.'

From *The Use of English* by Randolph Quirk

Exercise b

1   What does the writer mean by 'Received Pronunciation'?
2   Why would it be difficult to achieve a single standard pronunciation?
3   In what way is pronunciation like handwriting?
4   'Which', in line 19, refers to...

5   What is meant by 'and so on' in lines 27–8?

6   What changes are taking place in the position of Received Pronunciation, according to the writer?

Practice unit 6.3

Read the following text slowly and carefully and then answer the questions.

Sex and the Party

'What was she like, your wife?' said Julia.

'She was – do you know the Newspeak word *goodthinkful*? Meaning naturally orthodox, incapable of thinking a bad thought?'

'No, I didn't know the word, but I know the kind of person, right enough.'

He began telling her the story of his married life, but curiously enough she appeared   5
to know the essential parts of it already. She described to him, almost as though she had
seen or felt it, the stiffening of Katharine's body as soon as he touched her, the way in
which she still seemed to be pushing him from her with all her strength, even when her
arms were clasped tightly round him. With Julia he felt no difficulty in talking about
such things: Katharine, in any case, had long ceased to be a painful memory and   10
became merely a distasteful one.

'I could have stood it if it hadn't been for one thing,' he said. He told her about the
frigid little ceremony that Katharine had forced him to go through on the same night
every week. 'She hated it, but nothing would make her stop doing it. She used to call it –
but you'll never guess.'   15

'Our duty to the Party,' said Julia promptly.

'How did you know that?'

'I've been at school too, dear. Sex talks once a month for the over-sixteens. And in
the Youth Movement. They rub it into you for years. I dare say it works in a lot of
cases. But of course you can never tell; people are such hypocrites.'   20

She began to enlarge upon the subject. With Julia, everything came back to her own
sexuality. As soon as this was touched upon in any way she was capable of great acuteness.
Unlike Winston, she had grasped the inner meaning of the Party's sexual puritanism.
It was not merely that the sex instinct created a world of its own which was outside
the Party's control and which therefore had to be destroyed if possible. What was   25
more important was that sexual privation induced hysteria, which was desirable because it could be transformed into war-fever and leader-worship. The way she put it was:

'When you make love you're using up energy; and afterwards you feel happy and
don't give a damn for anything. They can't bear you to feel like that. They want you to
be bursting with energy all the time. All this marching up and down and cheering and   30
waving flags is simply sex gone sour. If you're happy inside yourself, why should you
get excited about Big Brother and the Three-Year Plans and the Two Minutes Hate and
all the rest of their bloody rot?'

That was very true, he thought. There was a direct intimate connexion between
chastity and political orthodoxy. For how could the fear, the hatred, and the lunatic   35
credulity which the Party needed in its members be kept at the right pitch, except by
bottling down some powerful instinct and using it as a driving force? The sex impulse
was dangerous to the Party, and the Party had turned it to account. They had played
a similar trick with the instinct of parenthood. The family could not actually be abolished,

and, indeed, people were encouraged to be fond of their children in almost the old-   40
fashioned way. The children, on the other hand, were systematically turned against their
parents and taught to spy on them and report their deviations. The family had become
in effect an extension of the Thought Police. It was a device by means of which everyone
could be surrounded night and day by informers who knew him intimately.

From *1984* by George Orwell

Exercise

1 Say, in one or two simple sentences, what was the Party's attitude to sex.
2 What is the implication of the expression 'curiously enough', in line 5?
3 Why did Julia already seem to know about Winston's wife?
4 Was he still living with his wife?
5 What does 'it' refer to in the expression 'I could have stood it' (line 12)?
6 What is 'that' in line 17?
7 Why does Julia use the word 'too' in line 18?
8 What is the second 'it' in line 19?
9 When Julia says 'You can never tell' (line 20), what is she referring to?
10 Give an alternative phrase for 'The way she put it', in line 27. (You can use the word 'way' if you wish.)
11 Who are 'they' in line 29?
12 What is meant by saying 'the Party had turned it to account' (line 38)?
13 Why was the sex impulse dangerous to the Party?
14 What was Julia's general attitude to political involvement?
15 What is 'it' in line 43?
16 What was the difference between the Party's attitude to parents and their treatment of children?
17 Who were the 'informers' (line 44)?

Teaching unit 7: Writing summaries

Read this text slowly and carefully, and then go on to the instructions and exercise which follow.

Progress in Samoa

Samoa Sasa sat cross-legged in his one-room, open-air home, shooing away chickens that strutted across the floor mats. Bananas cooked on the wood stove. Naked children cried in nearby huts. From one hut came the voice of Sinatra singing 'Strangers in the Night' on a local radio station.

The sound of progress frightened Sasa. For most of his 50 years time has stood   5
still. Now small European-styled homes are springing up around his village in Western Samoa and the young men are leaving for New Zealand. In the town there are experts from all over the world advising the Samoan Government on many development projects that Sasa does not understand.

The people of Luatuanuu Village – including his eight children – have always   10
worked the banana plantations and respected the custom that the Matais (family chiefs) like Sasa represented absolute authority.

They owned all the land communally, they elected a parliament and they adminis-
tered justice in each village, thus leaving few duties for the nation's 219-man police force.
Would all that, too, change? Sasa wondered.   15

'We are a poor country and change must come,' Sasa said through a translator. 'But I do
not want it so fast. I do not want my children to go to New Zealand to look for big money.
I want them to stay here in Luatuanuu and work our plantations as we always have done.'

The confusion Sasa feels is shared by many of the 150,000 Western Samoans – and
undoubtedly by the peoples of other newly independent, developing nations as well.   20
The capital, Apia, is teeming with people wanting to help: an 80-member US Peace
Corps headquarters, experts from the United Nations, investors from Japan, analysts
from the Asian Development Bank and civil engineers from New Zealand.

Already streets are being torn up for a new road system. The hospital is being rebuilt
with a loan from New Zealand. A new £1 million Government hotel has opened to   25
promote tourism – an industry the country is not quite sure it wants. A loan from the
Asian Development Bank will modernise the communications system. Japanese
investors have opened a sawmill and are building houses. When these and many other
development schemes are completed and Western Samoa, one of the world's poorest
nations in cash terms, is forced into the twentieth century, what is to become of its   30
culture?

'Most Samoans want the modern amenities, but they don't want to throw away our
culture to get them,' said Felise Va'a, editor of the *Samoan Times*. 'There is no easy
answer because in many ways our culture retards development. The question people
are asking is, what is a balance between the past and the future?'   35

The tradition of communal land ownership stultifies individual incentive and has
resulted in neglect of the land. The system of permitting only the nation's 15,000
Matais to elect 45 of the 47 MPs destroys political involvement. The exodus to New
Zealand – and the money the emigrants send home – creates a false economy and results
in thousands of Samoan families ignoring the land and living off the earnings of their   40
expatriate children.

New Zealand permits 1,500 Western Samoan immigrants a year and each year 1,500
– one per cent of the population – go. They, together with thousands of other Samoans
in New Zealand on temporary work visas, send home about £3 millions a year. The
money provides a boost to Western Samoa's agricultural economy, but it also is in-   45
flationary, and the inflation rate has been 35 per cent in two years.

Western Samoa has travelled a long way in the 12 years since independence. It has
political stability and a people who are 90 per cent literate. It offers investors a cheap
labour force, and a land that is 80 per cent uncultivated. It offers visitors the most un-
corrupted Polynesian culture left anywhere today.   50

Article in *The Guardian* by David Lamb

Suppose you had to answer the following question:

*In a paragraph of not more than 100 words, say what are the advantages and disadvantages of
progress from the Samoans' point of view.*
How would you go about it?

This type of test (often called summary) is not difficult if you follow a system. One
possible approach is to go through the following steps:

1   Read through the text from beginning to end, underlining all the points which should
    come into your answer. Do this very carefully, and be sure not to miss anything.

2 Make a list of notes, in which you reproduce very briefly in your own words all the points you have underlined. It might look like this:
   – Sasa frightened by progress
   – doesn't understand development
   – Samoa poor country, needs change
   – Sasa doesn't want change fast
   – doesn't want young people to emigrate
   – many other Samoans confused
   – Samoans want benefits of progress
   – but don't want to lose traditional culture
   – they want balance past and future
   – system of land ownership inefficient
   – electoral system undemocratic
   – money sent by emigrants good for economy
   – but causes inflation and neglect of land

   A good list is long from top to bottom (it has plenty of points in), but short from left to right (each point is expressed very briefly).

3 Without looking at the original text, join these points together into a paragraph. Change the order of the points if necessary, to make the construction more logical. Use conjunctions and adverbs such as 'therefore', 'however', 'although', 'since', to show the connections between the ideas.

Here is a possible paragraph:

Samoa is a very poor country with an inefficient system of land ownership and an undemocratic electoral system. Change is necessary; however, many Samoans, like Samoa Sasa, are worried about the speed of development. They want the benefits of progress, but find it difficult to understand what is happening, and are frightened of losing their traditional way of life. They do not want their young people to leave for New Zealand, and although the emigrants send money home, the increased wealth is causing neglect of the land and inflation. Samoa's problem is to find a compromise between past and future.

4 Look again at the text, just to check that you have not changed the meaning of anything; make corrections or rewrite the paragraph if necessary.

Exercise

Now try this question yourself: In a paragraph of not more than 100 words, describe the changes that are taking place in Samoa.

Practice unit 7.1

Read the text slowly and carefully and then answer the questions that follow.

The new music

The new music was built out of materials already in existence: blues, rock 'n' roll, folk music. But although the forms remained, something wholly new and original was made out of these older elements – more original, perhaps, than even the new musicians themselves yet realize. The transformation took place in 1966–7. Up to that

time, the blues had been an essentially black medium. Rock 'n' roll, a blues derivative,   5
was rhythmic, raunchy, teen-age dance music. Folk music, old and modern, was popular
among college students. The three forms remained musically and culturally distinct, and
even as late as 1965, none of them were expressing any radically new states of consciousness. Blues expressed black soul; rock, as made famous by Elvis Presley, was the beat of
youthful sensuality; and folk music, with such singers as Joan Baez, expressed anti-war   10
sentiments as well as the universal themes of love and disillusionment.

In 1966–7 there was a spontaneous transformation. In the United States, it originated
with youthful rock groups playing in San Francisco. In England, it was led by the Beatles,
who were already established as an extremely fine and highly individual rock group.
What happened, as well as it can be put into words, was this. First, the separate musical   15
traditions were brought together. Bob Dylan and the Jefferson Airplane played folk
rock, folk ideas with a rock beat. White rock groups began experimenting with the
blues. Of course, white musicians had always played the blues, but essentially as
imitators of the Negro style; now it began to be the white bands' own music. And
all of the groups moved towards a broader eclecticism* and synthesis. They freely took   20
over elements from Indian ragas, from jazz, from American country music, and as time
went on from even more diverse sources (one group seems recently to have been trying
out Gregorian chants). What developed was a protean music, capable of an almost limit-
less range of expression.

The second thing that happened was that all the musical groups began using the full   25
range of electric instruments and the technology of electronic amplifiers. The twangy
electric guitar was an old country–western standby, but the new electronic effects were
altogether different – so different that a new listener in 1967 might well feel that there
had never been any sounds like that in the world before. The high, piercing, unearthly
sounds of the guitar seemed to come from other realms. Electronics did, in fact, make   30
possible sounds that no instrument up to that time could produce. And in studio record-
ings, multiple tracking, feedback and other devices made possible effects that not even
an electronic band could produce live. Electronic amplification also made possible a
fantastic increase in volume, the music becoming as loud and penetrating as the human
ear could stand, and thereby achieving a 'total' effect, so that instead of an audience   35
of passive listeners, there were now audiences of total participants, feeling the music in all
of their senses and all of their bones.

Third, the music becomes a multi-media experience; a part of a total environment.
In the Bay Area ballrooms, the Fillmore, the Avalon, or Pauley Ballroom at the University of California, the walls were covered with fantastic changing patterns of light,   40
the beginning of the new art of the light show. And the audience did not sit, it danced.
With records at home, listeners imitated these lighting effects as best they could, and
heightened the whole experience by using drugs. Often music was played out of doors,
where nature – the sea or tall redwoods – provided the environment.

From *The Greening of America* by Charles Reich

Exercise

1   What were the 'three forms' referred to in line 7?
2   What is meant by 'culturally distinct' (line 7)?
3   What does 'them', in line 8, refer to?
4   What do you think is meant by 'new states of consciousness' (lines 8–9)?

* *eclecticism*: taking material from various sources

5 Give an alternative way of saying 'there was a spontaneous transformation' (line 12).
6 What was 'it' (line 13)?
7 Who started the change?
8 What was the difference in the white groups' attitudes to the blues before and after 1967?
9 What was 'it' (line 19)?
10 In line 25 we are told about 'the second thing that happened'. What was the first?
11 'The new electronic effects were altogether different' (lines 27–8). Different from what?
12 What is meant by the expression 'seemed to come from other realms' (line 30)?
13 What were the three different effects of the new electronic techniques, according to the passage?
14 What was the result of making the music very loud?
15 What is meant by 'the whole experience' (line 43)?
16 In a paragraph of not more than 100 words, sum up the changes that took place in music around 1966–7, according to the passage.

Practice unit 7.2

Read the text slowly and carefully and then answer the questions that follow.

Lie detector

A new form of lie detector that works by voice analysis and which can be used without a subject's knowledge has been introduced in Britain. The unit is already widely employed by the police and private industry in the US, and some of its applications there raise serious worries about its potential here. The Dektor psychological stress analyser (PSE) is used by private industry for pre-employment screening, investigating   5
thefts, and even periodic staff checks. Although at least 600 of the devices are used in the US, there are apparently only three in Britain. Burns International Security Services showed its PSE at the International Fire and Security Exhibition in London last week. Philip Hicks, assistant manager of Burns' Electron Division and the Burns official trained to use the PSE, said that one of the other two units was being employed by a private   10
firm for pre-employment checks.

In addition to the normally understood voice generation mechanisms – vibrations of the vocal chords and resonance of cavities inside the head – there is a third component caused by vibration of the muscles inside the mouth and throat. Normally, but not under stress, these voluntary muscles vibrate at 8–12 Hz, and this adds a clearly noticeable   15
frequency-modulated component to the voice. The PSE works by analysing this infrasonic FM component. Dektor claims that the muscle tightening occurs very quickly, and can change from one word to the next, so that it is possible to pick out a word or phrase that caused stress.

Dektor emphasises that the device shows only stress, not dishonesty. Three steps are   20
suggested to overcome this difficulty. First, the subject is supposed to see a full list of the questions in advance. Second, there are 'neutral' questions and one to which the subject is specifically asked to lie. Third, if an individual shows stress on a vital question (such as Have you stolen more than £100 in the last six months?), then additional questions must be asked to ensure that this does not reflect an earlier theft or the subject's know-   25
ledge of someone else responsible.

The standard report recommended by Dektor is simply the statement 'After careful analysis, it is the opinion of this Examiner that the Subject's chart did contain

specific reaction, indicative of deception, to the relevant questions listed below.' And
Hicks admitted that if a person showed stress and Hicks was unable to ascertain just   30
what caused the stress, he would assume that the stress was 'indicative of deception'.

In the US, the device is used for pre-employment interviews, with questions such as
'Have you used marihuana?', and for monthly checks with branch managers, asking
questions like 'Do you suspect any present employees of cheating the company?' –
which at least prevents a manager from setting his own pace to investigate possibly   35
suspicious behaviour. Finally, US insurance investigators are now using the PSE. They
need not carry it with them – only tape record the interview, usually with the permission
of the unsuspecting claimant. Not only does an assessor go through the claim form to
look for false claims (a questionable practice, because a person is just as likely to stress
over being reminded of a lost or damaged object as to lying), but he also offers less   40
money than requested. The claimant's response can, apparently, be analysed to show if
he is, in fact, likely to eventually accept.

The potential application of the PSE in Britain is extremely disquieting, especially as
there seems no law to prevent its use. The most serious problem is that its primary
application will be in situations where people may not object – such as pre-employment   45
interviews. But it can also be used to probe a whole range of personal issues totally
unrelated to a job – union and political affiliations, for example. And, of course, the
PSE can be used without the subject even knowing; its inventors analysed the televised
Watergate hearings and told the press who they thought was lying. Finally, the device
is not foolproof, but depends on the skill of the investigator, who receives only a one-   50
week course from Dektor.

In the US, where lie detectors of all sorts are much more widely used, Senator Sam
J. Ervin has introduced a bill to virtually prohibit their use by private companies. There
may be a privacy bill from the UK government this summer, and hopefully it will include
the use of lie detectors. In the interim, trade unions and consumer groups should prevent   55
their use before they become widespread.

Article by Joseph Hanlon in *New Scientist*

Exercise

1 Does the machine show whether a person is telling the truth?
2 What is meant by 'pre-employment screening'?
3 What happens in the throat and mouth, according to Dektor, when we say a word
   or expression that causes stress? (Answer as simply as possible.)
4 What is the relationship between Burns International Security Services and Dektor?
5 Does the machine analyse the whole of the sound of a person's voice?
6 Why is it suggested that subjects should be asked some neutral questions, and asked to
   lie in answer to one question?
7 How could a user of the machine make a mistake?
8 What is meant by 'setting his own pace' (line 35)?
9 How do investigators manage to use the machine without the subject knowing?
10 Why is it especially easy to make a mistake in an interview about an insurance claim?
11 What is meant by 'a questionable practice' (line 39)?
12 What is the implication of the word 'apparently' in line 41?
13 What might the claimant eventually accept (line 42)?
14 Rewrite in simpler language 'The potential application of the PSE in Britain is
    extremely disquieting'.

15 Read the sentence beginning 'The most serious problem' (lines 44–6) and explain briefly why this is the most serious problem.

16 In a paragraph of not more than 100 words, say what are the various ways in which this machine can be used, and what are the objections to its use.

Practice unit 7.3

Read the following text slowly and carefully and then answer the questions.

Dilemma of the working mother

Living with children is one of the few situations where virtue is rewarded. Though it sounds intolerably priggish to say so, parents who think first what's best for the children really do have an easier, more comfortable life than those who do what they like and make the children fit in.

The key decision is: should both parents go out to work? Dr Spock★ takes the standard 5 line: if a mother realises how vital her care is to a young baby 'it may make it easier for her to decide that the extra money she might earn, or the satisfaction she might receive from an outside job, is not so important after all'.

The evidence is, as usual, more confused. All research agrees on consistent loving care and a high level of stimulation as essential ingredients in optimal child development. 10 But there's increasing doubt that the 24 hours a day, seven days a week mum is the best way to provide it.

Two recent, as yet unpublished, London studies have quite independently come up with the same result: 40 per cent of mothers who stay at home with children under five are clinically depressed, although the depression is not necessarily caused by staying at 15 home. Dr Michael Rutter, of the Maudsley Hospital, and Dr G. Stewart Prince, among others, have shown that depressed mothers produce depressed, neurotic and backward children. There are many other mothers who, without being depressed, are *oppressed* by the unending repetitive task of caring for a young baby, or the unceasing chatter of a toddler, and so get less pleasure from their children than they 20 might.

Extra money is not to be despised. It buys automatic washers, tumble driers, dish-washers to make life easier and give more real attention-time to the children. It buys time off, excursions, holidays. It may make the difference between a town flat and a house with a garden, a better environment for bringing up children. 25

For professional women there is another difficulty. To give up or even work part-time, probably means climbing painfully back on to the bottom rung of the ladder at 35 or 40 in galling subordination to younger and perhaps less able men.

Assuming the still-normal situation – mother at home – there are ways to guard against the imprisoned feeling. Any arrangement will do as long as it's regular and 30 doesn't involve renegotiation every time.

For instance, once a week, a completely free day and evening during which the mother is relieved of all responsibility. She can visit friends, or go to a museum, spend all morning buying a pair of shoes and needn't come back until she feels like it. The only rule is she must go out, not hang around catching up on household jobs. It's best of all 35 if combined with a regular night out for parents together. You can employ another

★ *Dr Spock*: author of a well-known book on child care

woman to stand in for the day, set up a reciprocal arrangement with another family, or make it a Saturday when Father can take over – but that's less good.

The split Saturday works well for some families. Father has morning off, Mother afternoon, to do what they like unencumbered by children. Much nicer for them, too, than the family shopping expedition, which soon makes small children tired and fractious. 40

Child-free weekends every few months are very restorative, and well worth the money. Family exchanges are fun for older children. Advertise if you don't know a suitable family, but get well acquainted before you go off. 45

A word of caution: work which can be done at home is superficially attractive – Rhona and Robert Rapport's book *Dual-Career Families* describes several households coping with this situation. But there is good evidence that withdrawal of attention is more harmful to children than physical absence – which is one reason why the switch-off phenomenon associated with maternal depression is so damaging. 50

Anyone with a toddler knows how he will play happily while you cook, wash up or make beds, but no sooner do you sit down with a book, pick up a complicated piece of knitting or take out your violin than he becomes demanding and tiresome. In our house 'Mum's writing an article' is a signal for unusual gloom, whereas 'Mum's off for the weekend' is excellent news. (But it's not a good idea to leave a child for very long between the ages of 9 months and 2.) 55

Article in *The Observer* Magazine

Exercise

1 The writer suggests that parents who 'think first what's best for the children' have an easier life. Why do you think this is likely to be so?
2 What does the expression 'the key decision' mean?
3 What is meant by 'Dr Spock takes the standard line' (lines 5–6)?
4 What is more important, according to Dr Spock, than 'the extra money she might earn' (line 7)?
5 What does the writer feel about Dr Spock's view?
6 What is 'it' in line 12?
7 Why is it suggested that full-time mothers may be unable to care for their children properly?
8 In what ways, according to the writer, might a working mother be able to give more real care to her child?
9 'For professional women there is another difficulty' (line 26). What is the first?
10 What does the writer mean by 'climbing painfully back on to the bottom rung of the ladder' (line 27)?
11 What does 'it' in line 30 refer to?
12 What does 'it' in line 35 refer to?
13 Give an alternative phrase for 'Get well acquainted before you go off' (line 45).
14 What is the problem about work that can be done at home?
15 Explain 'the switch-off phenomenon associated with maternal depression' (lines 49–50).
16 In a paragraph of not more than 100 words, sum up the various things a mother of small children can do (according to the writer) in order not to be trapped and oppressed by her family.

Practice unit 7.4

Read the text slowly and carefully and then answer the questions that follow.

Rescue archaeology in Scotland

Scottish history is being lost irretrievably and at a critical rate beneath the earthmovers and cement beds of redevelopment. That fact has emerged from meetings at Perth and St Andrews during the past few days called by Rescue, the Trust for British Archaeology.

More than seventy historic Scottish towns are thought by archaeologists to be threatened with Perth and St Andrews principal among them. In the countryside thousands of sites,   5 from the earliest prehistoric middens to the remains of the last century, lie unexplored.

Before the seventeenth century, they explained, documentary evidence about Scottish communities was sparse. The country did not have the same conscientious habit as medieval England of recording its history.

Dr Nicholas Brooks, of St Andrews University, declared: 'The first five centuries of   10 Scottish town history relies almost entirely on archaeological work to show the pattern of trade, defences, the type of housing and churches, the social habits and the health of the people living there. It is archaeology that tells us how they lived, what they ate and how they died.'

Last year only five towns of 77 needing investigation had rescue work carried out on   15 them and a mere £25,000 of the £1m British budget for rescue archaeology was spent in Scotland. In relation to size and population the country has a far higher proportion of ancient monuments under state guardianship than England but the trained archaeo-logical officers able to organize rescue operations ahead of the bulldozer number barely a handful.
  20

The council of the Society of Antiquaries of Scotland has recommended that 20 such officers should work on the new regional authorities to assess sites and provide the liaison between developers and local authorities. That would also provide better career prospects for trained archaeologists in Scotland.

Rescue regards that as an excellent first step. It has proposed an immediate survey at   25 Perth, where redevelopment is to take place on a plot overlapping the site of the original Scottish Parliament.

In St Andrews, where little has changed during the past 300 years, archaeologists detect sinister signs. 'The town centre is a conservation area and St Andrews has its own planning authority, but it is calculated that in the past decade one tenth of the medieval   30 borough has been destroyed by piecemeal development. All hope of recovering information has been lost', Dr Brooks says.

The difficulty lies in the ruthless strength of modern machines used to plough up or clear the ground, to drive in the supporting piles or peel back an opencast coal mine. The Society of Antiquaries complains that much has already gone.
  35

Road metal is being quarried from one of the largest and most important native hill forts in Britain at Traprain Law, East Lothian. One of the best preserved Roman marching camps in Scotland was recently ploughed up.

Scotland has about 75,000 known field monuments. About three quarters of them are unprotected. 'As long as change was fairly leisurely, Scotland's archaeology was   40 reasonably secure. That is no longer so and an alarm must be sounded.'

Report in *The Times*

Exercise

1   Why is Scottish history being lost?
2   What is meant by 'at a critical rate' (line 1)?
3   'Them', in line 5, refers to...
4   Why is archaeology especially important for Scotland?
5   'They', in line 7, refers to...
6   What does 'its', in line 9, refer to?
7   Where is 'there', in line 13?
8   Who are 'they' in lines 13–14?
9   What kind of information can archaeology give us about Scottish history, according to the passage?
10 What is strange about the way the money available for rescue archaeology in Britain is spent?
11 What does 'them', in line 16, refer to?
12 What are the difficulties in the way of rescue archaeology in Scotland?
13 Rewrite the following extract so as to express the meaning in another way (you do not have to change *all* the words): 'the trained archaeological officers able to organize rescue operations ahead of the bulldozer number barely a handful' (lines 18–20).
14 What does 'it' refer to, in line 25?
15 What sort of information is referred to in line 32?
16 '...much has already gone' (line 35). Much what?
17 What is 'no longer so' (line 41)?
18 In a short paragraph of not more than 100 words, sum up the present situation of Scottish rescue archaeology and the action that has been suggested.

Practice unit 7.5

Read the text carefully and then answer the questions that follow.

The causes of conflict

The evidence taken from the observation of the behavior of apes and children suggests that there are three clearly separable groups of simple causes for the outbreak of fighting and the exhibition of aggressiveness by individuals.

One of the most common causes of fighting among both children and apes was over the *possession* of external objects. The disputed ownership of any desired object – food,   5
clothes, toys, females, and the affection of others – was sufficient ground for an appeal to force. On Monkey Hill disputes over females were responsible for the death of thirty out of thirty-three females. Two points are of particular interest to notice about these fights for possession.

In the first place they are often carried to such an extreme that they end in the   10
complete destruction of the objects of common desire. Toys are torn to pieces. Females are literally torn limb from limb. So overriding is the aggression once it has begun that it not only overflows all reasonable boundaries of selfishness but utterly destroys the object for which the struggle began and even the self for whose advantage the struggle was undertaken.   15

In the second place it is observable, at least in children, that the object for whose possession aggression is started may sometimes be desired by one person only or merely because it is desired by someone else. There were many cases observed by Dr Isaacs where toys and other objects which had been discarded as useless were violently defended by their owners when they became the object of some other child's desire. The grounds of possessiveness may, therefore, be irrational in the sense that they are derived from inconsistent judgments of value. Whether sensible or irrational, contests over possession are commonly the occasion for the most ruthless use of force among children and apes. 20

One of the commonest kinds of object arousing possessive desire is the notice, good will, affection, and service of other members of the group. Among children one of the commonest causes of quarreling was 'jealousy' – the desire for the exclusive possession of the interest and affection of someone else, particularly the adults in charge of the children. This form of behavior is sometimes classified as a separate cause of conflict under the name of 'rivalry' or 'jealousy'. But, in point of fact, it seems to us that it is only one variety of possessiveness. The object of desire is not a material object – that is the only difference. The object is the interest and affection of other persons. What is wanted, however, is the exclusive right to that interest and affection – a property in emotions instead of in things. As subjective emotions and as causes of conflict, jealousy and rivalry are fundamentally similar to the desire for the uninterrupted possession of toys or food. Indeed, very often the persons, property which is desired, are the sources of toys and food. 25 30 35

Possessiveness is, then, in all its forms a common cause of fighting. If we are to look behind the mere facts of behavior for an explanation of this phenomenon, a teleological cause* is not far to seek. The exclusive right to objects of desire is a clear and simple advantage to the possessor of it. It carries with it the certainty and continuity of satisfaction. Where there is only one claimant to a good, frustration and the possibility of loss is reduced to a minimum. It is, therefore, obvious that, if the ends of the self are the only recognized ends, the whole powers of the agent, including the fullest use of his available force, will be used to establish and defend exclusive rights to possession. 40

Another cause of aggression closely allied to possessiveness is the tendency for children and apes greatly to resent the *intrusion of a stranger* into their group. A new child in the class may be laughed at, isolated, and disliked and even set upon and pinched and bullied. A new monkey may be poked and bitten to death. It is interesting to note that it is only strangeness within a similarity of species that is resented. Monkeys do not mind being joined by a goat or a rat. Children do not object when animals are introduced to the group. Indeed, such novelties are often welcomed. But when monkeys meet a new monkey or children a strange child, aggression often occurs. This suggests strongly that the reason for the aggression is fundamentally possessiveness. The competition of the newcomers is feared. The present members of the group feel that there will be more rivals for the food or the attention of the adults. 45 50 55

Finally, another common source of fighting among children is a failure or *frustration* in their own activity. A child will be prevented either by natural causes such as bad weather or illness or by the opposition of some adult from doing something he wishes to do at a given moment – sail his boat or ride the bicycle. The child may also frustrate itself by failing, through lack of skill or strength, to complete successfully some desired activity. Such a child will then in the ordinary sense become 'naughty.' He will be in a bad or surly temper. And, what is of interest from our point of view, the child will indulge in aggression – attacking and fighting other children or adults. Sometimes the object of aggression will simply be the cause of frustration, a straightforward reaction. The child will kick or hit the nurse who forbids the sailing of his boat. But sometimes – 60 65

* *a teleological cause*: an explanation in terms of purpose

indeed, frequently – the person or thing that suffers the aggression is quite irrelevant and innocent of offense. The angry child will stamp the ground or box the ears of another child when neither the ground nor the child attacked is even remotely connected with the irritation or frustration.

Of course, this kind of behavior is so common that everyone feels it to be obvious and to constitute no serious scientific problem. That a small boy should pull his sister's hair because it is raining does not appear to the ordinary unreflecting person to be an occasion for solemn scientific inquiry. He is, as we should all say, 'in a bad temper.' Yet it is not, in fact, really obvious either why revenge should be taken on entirely innocent objects, since no good to the aggressor can come of it, or why children being miserable should seek to make others miserable also. It is just a fact of human behavior that cannot really be deduced from any general principle of reason. But it is, as we shall see, of very great importance for our purpose. It shows how it is possible, at the simplest and most primitive level, for aggression and fighting to spring from an entirely irrelevant and partially hidden cause. Fighting to possess a desired object is straightforward and rational, however disastrous its consequences, compared with fighting that occurs because, in a different and unrelated activity, some frustration has barred the road to pleasure. The importance of this possibility for an understanding of group conflict must already be obvious.

From 'Personal Aggressiveness and War' by E. F. M. Durbin and John Bowlby

Exercise

1 What was the purpose of the observations of apes and children described in the passage?
2 What is meant by 'others' in line 6?
3 Give an alternative phrase for 'the objects of common desire' (line 11).
4 What is meant by 'it...utterly destroys...even the self for whose advantage the struggle was undertaken' (lines 13–15)?
5 What is 'it' in line 18?
6 Who or what are 'they' in line 20?
7 Why does the author think that jealousy is not a completely separate cause of conflict?
8 Explain the meaning of 'the object' (line 30)?
9 What is meant by 'strangeness within a similarity of species' (line 49)?
10 What are 'such novelties' (line 51)?
11 Explain simply 'a failure or frustration in their own activity' (lines 56–7).
12 What does the writer mean by 'the object of aggression' (line 64)?
13 Does the writer suggest a reason why people take revenge on innocent objects?
14 What does 'it' refer to in line 77?
15 Why does the writer regard the observation discussed in the last paragraph as especially important?
16 What is 'our purpose' (line 78)?
17 In a paragraph of not more than 100 words, sum up what the writer says about the causes of conflict.

Section C:
Perception of the effective use of English

Teaching unit 8: Appreciation of a writer's use of language 1

The way in which a writer uses language is always important: if he does not choose his words carefully and organise his sentences well, what he writes may be unclear or ineffective. This is particularly true of certain kinds of writing, in which the style itself is sometimes a vital part of the meaning. For instance, a novel, a humorous article, a political manifesto or an advertisement may depend very largely for its effect on how the writer expresses himself; his choice and arrangement of words can become even more important than what he says. Comprehension questions in examinations sometimes test your ability to observe and describe a writer's technique. It is not, of course, necessary to be a student of literature in order to deal with questions of this kind. However, you need to be able to see (and say) why an author chooses a certain word or expression, rather than another with a similar meaning, and it is also useful to be familiar with common stylistic devices such as irony, repetition, variation of style, use of comparisons, etc. This unit and the ones which follow will give you practice in picking out and explaining points of this sort.

Exercise

Read this text slowly and carefully. Decide what you think was the author's purpose in writing it, and then answer the questions that follow.

Firm friends of ours

We've just had another of our regular visits from Christopher and Lavinia Crumble, our private consumer research, marriage guidance, home heating, and child welfare advisory service.

They come in about once a month and straighten us out. What I admire about them is their tremendous firmness in dealing with us. It's no good just offering vague suggestions   5
to feckless problem families like us. You've got to tell us exactly what to do, and then you've to damn well stand over us and make sure we do it.

With their great sense of social responsibility and their unbounded moral energy, the Crumbles usually set to work even before they are through the front door.

'I see you've still got one of these old-fashioned locks,' says Christopher. 'You realise   10
that any half-wit burglar could pick this with a bent pin and a nail-file in about five seconds flat? Couldn't he, darling?'

'Christopher will give you the address of the firm that imports those new draught-proof Swiss micro-precision locks,' says Lavinia. 'Won't you, darling?'

'Oh, I'll give their local office a ring tomorrow and get them to send you a fitter round   15
right away. No, no – no trouble at all. Is it darling?'

Christopher has scarcely had time to make a note in his diary before Lavinia has stepped
back in amazement. Oh God, the doormat! We've forgotten about the doormat!

'You *said* you were going to get one of those hand-knitted Vietnamese ones like
ours,' says Lavinia. 'Didn't they darling? What happened? I mean, goodness   20
knows, it's your home – it's up to you to decide what sort of doormat you want in it.
But when it's been scientifically *proved* by independent experts that the hand-knitted ones
have by far the highest mat–sole abrasion co-efficient . . . !'

By the time we sit down to dinner the Crumbles have already put our domestic
economy right on a number of points, and it's the turn of my wife's cooking for a help-   25
ing hand. But the tact they do it with!

'This apple-pie is absolutely marvellous, isn't it, darling?'

'Marvellous!'

'*Marvellous!* Of course we've rather gone off having heavy pastry dishes on top of
great, greasy meals – haven't we, darling? – and I've got a wonderful new recipe for   30
mango sorbet that you absolutely *must* try.'

'We think it's the *only* pudding in the world, don't we, darling?'

'Though, of course, we *adore* apple-pie, too.'

It also turns out in the course of conversation – and this we had not known or
suspected before – that we are absolutely obliged to read Ned Ogham's new novel   35
(which Lavinia will send us) about a Midlands couple who keep a chicken grill, and
who barbecue a passing encyclopædia salesman in the Rotisso-mat as a sacrifice to the
sun-god. We are under a further categorical imperative to see Fred Umble's new play
(Christopher will get us the tickets) about a group of workers in an expanded poly-
styrene factory who ritually beat the tea-girl to death with plastic spoons, and eat her   40
for lunch in a Dionysiac frenzy in the works canteen.

And what about the floor? Do we like it the way it is? inquires Christopher with the
old tact. Or shall he bring over the five-gallon drum of Simpson's 'Florscraypa' they
happen to have left from doing their lavatory, so we can really get down on our hands
and knees this week-end and start all over again?   45

'Of course,' says Lavinia, 'it would make all the difference to the room if the *ceiling*
were brightened up a bit, wouldn't it, darling?'

'They'd be far better off with *something* on the ceiling, certainly. How about
wallpaper!'

'*Yes!* One of those rather William Morrissy ones!'   50

'That's a tremendously exciting idea, darling. We'll pop along to that little man of
ours in Muswell Hill to-morrow and see what he's got.'

'Then we could throw out that ghastly old sofa and get a chaise-longue. We could
cover it with one of those rather art-nouveauish prints, couldn't we, darling?'

They're also going to get our children into a marvellous pre-nursery school that   55
all our friends use, with a very high pass rate into the top nursery schools in the district,
though whether to send them now or after the Christmas exam season they haven't
quite decided yet. They don't think there's any need to worry too much about the
children's development, we're relieved to hear, provided we treat them as rational
human beings, on a man-to-man basis, the way the Crumbles would treat their own   60
children, if they had any.

'Or course, what children need most,' explains Lavinia, 'as psychiatrists now agree,
is a constructively disturbed home background.'

'As I expect you know,' smiles Christopher, 'the really well-adjusted couples
aren't the ones who are so suspiciously polite and loving to one another all the time.   65
Are they, darling?'

'No – the really well-adjusted couples are the ones who fight like cat and dog at every opportunity. We have the most tremendously helpful fights, don't we, darling?'

'Oh, all the time. We were just thinking the other day – weren't we, darling? – that whenever we see you two you scarcely so much as say a word to each other. It's very bad to bottle it all up, you know. If you want to have a bit of a scrap, you go ahead. We don't mind. Do we, darling?' 70

Heavens, we're grateful for all they've done for us. About the only service left unperformed is to tell us that of course our breath smells *marvellous*, but we absolutely *must* try a wonderful little deodorant toothpaste they know about... 75

How about it, darlings?

From *At Bay in Gear Street* by Michael Frayn

1 The writer describes the Crumbles as 'our private consumer research, marriage guidance, home heating, and child welfare advisory service'. This makes them sound very knowledgeable and important. Do you think he describes them in this way
a) because he admires them? If so, why?
b) because he is being ironic, and means something else? If so, what?
c) because he wishes to write in a very literary style? If so, why?

2 Which of the following extracts from the passage seem to you to be ironic?
a) 'What I admire about them is their tremendous firmness in dealing with us.' (lines 4–5)
b) 'With their great sense of social responsibility...' (line 8)
c) 'Christopher has scarcely had time to make a note in his diary before Lavinia has stepped back in amazement' (lines 17–18)
d) '...it's the turn of my wife's cooking for a helping hand' (lines 25–6)
e) 'But the tact they do it with!' (line 26)
f) 'Then we could throw out that ghastly old sofa and get a chaise-longue' (line 53)
g) 'It's very bad to bottle it all up, you know' (lines 70–1)
h) 'Heavens, we're grateful...' (line 73)

3 In lines 29–33, four words are printed in italics. What do you think is the best explanation for this?
a) because these words are said louder
b) because these words are more important
c) to show something of the Crumbles' character by the way they emphasise words

4 Expressions like 'Couldn't he, darling?', 'Won't you, darling?', occur several times in the passage. Do you think
a) this is just the way the Crumbles talk?
b) it is a stylistic habit of the writer?
c) it is to show that the Crumbles love each other?
d) it is for another reason? If so, what?

5 The writer expresses himself quite forcefully in the phrases 'feckless problem families like us' and 'you've to damn well stand over us and make sure we do it' (lines 6, 7). Is he representing
a) the reader's attitude?
b) his own attitude?
c) the Crumbles' attitude?

6　Why is 'said' printed in italics (line 19)?
a)　Because they didn't buy the doormat after all.
b)　Because Lavinia is excited.
c)　Because it is an important word.

7　The sentence beginning 'But when it's been scientifically proved...' (line 22) is unfinished. Can you suggest how it might have continued?

8　What is the writer's purpose in making Lavinia refer to such strange objects as 'draught-proof Swiss micro-precision locks' and 'hand-knitted Vietnamese doormats'?

9　In lines 53–4, what is the writer's purpose in using the pronoun 'we'?

10　'A marvellous pre-nursery school that all our friends use, with a very high pass rate into the top nursery schools in the district' (lines 55–6). Comment on the writer's satirical intention.

11　Is the phrase 'we're relieved to hear', in line 59, intended to be taken literally or not?

12　The phrase 'if they had any', in line 61, obviously implies that the Crumbles have no children. Does it have any further implication?

13　What do you feel is the writer's main intention in this passage?
a)　To describe his friends the Crumbles.
b)　To amuse the reader by satirising a certain kind of person.
c)　To explain to the reader the problems he has with his friends.
d)　To make the reader feel concerned about his problems.
e)　To communicate his view of life.

Practice unit 8.1

Read the text slowly and carefully and then answer the questions which follow.

Traveller's tales

My wife and I found out quite a lot about England while we were in America; and we've found out a thing or two about America since we've been back in England.

　　Various people have asked us what America was like, and then, when we've floundered about hopelessly, mumbling that it was big, have kindly come to our rescue and told us, often telling us what we thought of the place as well. We enjoyed visiting it, but　　　5
we shouldn't like to live there; that seems to be the consensus of opinion – a conclusion that satisfies pretty well everyone.

　　Our good friends Christopher and Lavinia Crumble have been particularly helpful, as they always are when it comes to knowing what to think about a thing.

　　'What you must have found so dreadful was the whole pace of life over there,　　　10
I should think,' says Christopher. 'Wouldn't you, darling?'

　　'Oh, you must have found it a perpetual strain,' says Lavinia. 'Mustn't they, darling?'

　　I cast my mind back desperately, trying to focus it on the Pace of American Life.
'Well,' I begin cautiously.

　　'I mean,' says Christopher, 'I gather the social pressures are tremendous, for a start.'　　　15
Social Pressures. Now, let's think, did I come across a Social Pressure? 'Well,' I venture.

　　'And the strains of commuting,' says Lavinia. 'Which is something that seems absolutely appalling to us, because as you know we are very committed to the idea of actually living in town – aren't we, darling? – which I know is unheard of in America.'

　　'Oh, well...'　　　20

'And slipping away at weekends to our little place in the country,' says Christopher. 'Which I suppose is something the Americans don't have at all, since it's entirely occupied by all those immense suburban housing developments...'

'And if there's one thing I should hate,' says Lavinia, 'it would be to find myself stuck in a suburban ranch-type house surrounded by nothing but shiny domestic 25 gadgets, and housewives committing adultery and going mad from boredom and frustration.'

Oh God! I see it all now! We met the wrong lot of housewives! We went to the wrong lot of houses!

'Of course,' says Christopher. 'Life is a dreadful rat-race over there altogether. The 30 trouble is that Americans are so tremendously conformist. Aren't they, darling?'

'Oh, if you express any sort of dissent at all you're automatically branded as a Communist. Aren't you, darling?'

The Rat Race! That's what I should have been looking at! The Conformism! All the people getting branded as Communists! Bitterly regret all the time we spent knocking 35 around with people who expressed the most radical dissent on every subject, and who totally failed to get themselves branded as Communists at all.

'How did you get on with all that air-conditioning?' asks Christopher with a smile.

Well, I begin, when we arrived the thermometer was in the eighties, with very high humidity and we were extremely glad of... 40

'I suppose with their mania about personal cleanliness', says Lavinia, 'they were all dashing off to take showers every five minutes?'

Well, when the temperature's 80 or 90, and the humidity is ...

'How did you get on with the food over there?' laughs Christopher. 'You must be quite pleased to see decent fruit and vegetables again, after all the flavourless, pre- 45 packaged stuff you get over there. Mustn't they, darling?'

I start to explain that by some unfortunate local atypicality, the fruit and vegetables we came across were in fact better than English fruit and vegetables. But already we're on to American children. It turns out we met the wrong lot of American children, too! All the ones we met were delightful, which just goes to show the dangers of generalizing 50 from one's own limited experience, because the Crumbles are able to assure us categorically that American children are in fact unbearable.

Anyway, they're sure we're glad to be back. And as they say, it's marvellous to hear at first hand exactly what America is like. Particularly since it turns out to be so much like they'd always supposed. 55

From *At Bay in Gear Street* by Michael Frayn

Exercise

1 Can you give two examples of expressions used ironically in the passage?
2 Comment on the fact that several sentences in the conversation are unfinished.
3 'We enjoyed visiting it, but we shouldn't like to live there' (lines 5–6). Whose opinion is this?
4 In line 11, Christopher says 'Wouldn't you, darling?' Who is this addressed to?
5 Comment on the use of the word 'must' in lines 10, 12, 44 and 46.
6 When the writer talks about 'the dangers of generalizing from one's own limited experience' (lines 50–1), what is he suggesting?
7 Explain the implication of the last sentence in the passage.
8 What do you think is the writer's purpose?

Practice unit 8.2

Read the text slowly and carefully and then answer the questions that follow.

The fish dream

'I think your dream is charming', said Major Sanderson, the psychiatrist, with a sharp, nervous laugh, 'and I hope it recurs frequently so that we can continue discussing it. Would you like a cigarette?' He smiled when Yossarian declined. 'Just why do you think,' he asked knowingly, 'that you have such a strong aversion to accepting a cigarette from me?'

'I put one out a second ago. It's still smoldering in your ash tray.'   5

Major Sanderson chuckled. 'That's a very ingenious explanation. But I suppose we'll soon discover the true reason.' He tied a sloppy double bow in his opened shoelace and then transferred a lined yellow pad from his desk to his lap. 'This fish you dream about. Let's talk about that. It's always the same fish, isn't it?'

'I don't know,' Yossarian replied. 'I have trouble recognizing fish.'   10

'What does the fish remind you of?'

'Other fish.'

'And what do other fish remind you of?'

'Other fish.'

Major Sanderson sat back disappointedly. 'Do you like fish?'   15

'Not especially.'

'Just why do you think you have such a morbid aversion to fish?' asked Major Sanderson triumphantly.

'They're too bland,' Yossarian answered. 'And too bony.'

Major Sanderson nodded understandingly, with a smile that was agreeable and   20
insincere. 'That's a very interesting explanation. But we'll soon discover the true reason, I suppose. Do you like this particular fish? The one you're holding in your hand?'

'I have no feelings about it either way.'

'Do you dislike the fish? Do you have any hostile or aggressive emotions   25
towards it?'

'No, not at all. In fact, I rather like the fish.'

'Then you do like the fish.'

'Oh no. I have no feelings toward it either way.'

'But you just said you liked it. And now you say you have no feelings toward it   30
either way. I've just caught you in a contradiction. Don't you see?'

'Yes, sir. I suppose you have caught me in a contradiction.'

Major Sanderson proudly lettered 'Contradiction' on his pad with his thick black pencil. 'Just why do you think,' he resumed when he had finished, looking up, 'that you made those two statements expressing contradictory emotional responses to the   35
fish?'

'I suppose I have an ambivalent attitude toward it.'

Major Sanderson sprang up with joy when he heard the words 'ambivalent attitude'. 'You do understand!' he exclaimed, wringing his hands together ecstatically. 'Oh, you can't imagine how lonely it's been for me, talking day after day to patients who   40
haven't the slightest knowledge of psychiatry, trying to cure people who have no real interest in me or my work! I'd like to show you some ink blots now to find out what certain shapes and colors remind you of.'

'You can save yourself the trouble, Doctor. Everything reminds me of sex.'

'Does it?' cried Major Sanderson with delight, as though unable to believe his ears.   45
'Now we're *really* getting somewhere! Do you ever have any good sex dreams?'

'My fish dream is a sex dream.'

'No, I mean real sex dreams – the kind where you grab some naked bitch by the neck and pinch her and punch her in the face until she's all bloody and then throw yourself down to ravish her and burst into tears because you love her and hate her so much   50
you don't know what else to do. *That's* the kind of sex dreams I like to talk about. Don't you ever have sex dreams like that?'

Yossarian reflected a moment with a wise look. 'That's a fish dream,' he decided.

From *Catch-22* by Joseph Heller

Exercise

1   The following expressions are used to describe the psychiatrist's behaviour during the interview: he smiled (line 3); he asked knowingly (line 4); chuckled (line 6); triumphantly (line 18); proudly (line 33). What do these expressions tell us about Major Sanderson's attitude?

2   Why did he 'sit back disappointedly' (line 15)?

3   Why was his smile 'agreeable and insincere' (lines 20–1)?

4   Why was he pleased when Yossarian said he had an 'ambivalent attitude' (line 37)?

5   What is the significance of 'do' in 'You do understand' (line 39)?

6   Why does Major Sanderson say 'Now we're *really* getting somewhere' (line 46)?

7   Why are there no commas in the long sentence from 'the kind...' to '...what else to do' (lines 48–51)?

8   Comment on the expression 'That's a fish dream'. What effect do you think it has on Major Sanderson? And what effect do you think it is meant to have on the reader?

9   What do you think is the writer's main purpose in this passage?

Practice unit 8.3

Read the text slowly and carefully, and then answer the questions that follow.

The painter

He really was an impossible person. Too shy altogether. With absolutely nothing to say for himself. And such a weight. Once he was in your studio he never knew when to go, but would sit on and on until you nearly screamed, and burned to throw something enormous after him when he did finally blush his way out – something like the tortoise stove. The strange thing was that at first sight he looked most interesting. Everybody   5
agreed about that. You would drift into the café one evening and there you would see, sitting in a corner, with a glass of coffee in front of him, a thin dark boy, wearing a blue jersey with a little grey flannel jacket buttoned over it. And somehow that blue jersey and the grey jacket with the sleeves that were too short gave him the air of a boy that has made up his mind to run away to sea. Who has run away in fact, and will get up   10
in a moment and sling a knotted handkerchief containing his nightshirt and his mother's picture on the end of a stick, and walk out into the night and be drowned...Stumble over the wharf edge on his way to the ship, even...He had black close-cropped hair,

grey eyes with long lashes, white cheeks and a mouth pouting as though he were
determined not to cry...How could one resist him? Oh, one's heart was wrung at sight. 15
And, as if that were not enough, there was his trick of blushing...Whenever the waiter
came near him he turned crimson – he might have been just out of prison and the
waiter in the know...

    'Who is he, my dear? Do you know?'

    'Yes. His name is Ian French. Painter. Awfully clever, they say. Someone started 20
by giving him a mother's tender care. She asked him how often he heard from home,
whether he had enough blankets on his bed, how much milk he drank a day. But when
she went round to his studio to give an eye to his socks, she rang and rang, and though
she could have sworn she heard someone breathing inside, the door was not
answered...Hopeless!' 25

    Someone else decided that he ought to fall in love. She summoned him to her side,
called him 'boy', leaned over him so that he might smell the enchanting perfume of
her hair, took his arm, told him how marvellous life could be if one only had the
courage, and went round to his studio one evening and rang and rang...Hopeless.

    'What the poor boy really wants is thoroughly rousing,' said a third. So off they 30
went to cafés and cabarets, little dances, places where you drank something that tasted
like tinned apricot juice, but cost twenty-seven shillings a bottle and was called
champagne, other places, too thrilling for words, where you sat in the most awful
gloom, and where someone had always been shot the night before. But he did not
turn a hair. Only once he got very drunk, but instead of blossoming forth, there he sat, 35
stony, with two spots of red on his cheeks, like, my dear, yes, the dead image of that
rag-time thing they were playing, like a 'Broken Doll'. But when she took him back
to his studio he had quite recovered, and said 'good night' to her in the street below, as
though they had walked home from church together...Hopeless.

    After heaven knows how many more attempts – for the spirit of kindness dies very 40
hard in women – they gave him up. Of course, they were still perfectly charming, and
asked him to their shows, and spoke to him in the café but that was all. When one is an
artist one has no time simply for people who won't respond. Has one?

From *Feuille d'Album* by Katherine Mansfield

Exercise

1   The first few sentences of the passage have a special kind of structure. What do you
    think is the reason for this?
a) It is done for emphasis.
b) It is meant to reflect the fragmented personality of the true artist.
c) It makes the style more vivid.
d) It gives the impression of direct speech.
2   Who does 'you', in line 3, refer to?
3   Comment on the choice of the word 'burned' in line 3.
4   Comment on the expression 'blush his way out', in line 4.
5   Why does the author say 'drift', in line 6, instead of 'go'?
6   In the section from lines 30 to 39, what expressions make the reader feel that it is really
    a passage of direct speech?
7   Who are 'they' in line 41?
8   'When one is an artist one has no time simply for people who won't respond. Has one?'
    (lines 42–3). Who seems to be talking to whom in this extract?

9 Do you think that the style of the passage is intended principally to give us a picture of the personality of
a) the author?
b) the women who were interested in the boy?
c) the boy himself?

Teaching unit 9: Appreciation of a writer's use of language 2

When Julius Caesar wanted an impressive way to describe his successful invasion of Britain, he chose the sentence 'veni, vidi, vici' (I came, I saw, I conquered). This phrase is obviously very effective – perhaps for two main reasons. First, it is very short, which somehow helps to give the impression that Caesar's conquest of Britain must have been quick and efficient. And secondly, the three words are all of the same length, and they begin and end with the same letter, so that when used together they create an almost musical effect - the sentence sounds good.

Writers who want to make their subject matter sound 'special' (beautiful, impressive, mysterious, etc.) often use particular kinds of sentence structure which contribute to the effect. For instance, a writer may build a paragraph out of sentences which are all divided into two or three equal parts; or he may deliberately alternate long and short sentences; or he may choose his words and expressions not only because of their meaning but also for the sake of their sound.

Repetition of words and structures can be very effective. We are usually told at school not to begin all our sentences in the same way (and especially not to begin all our sentences with 'I'), and it is certainly true that careless repetitions can be monotonous. However, when important words or phrases are repeated deliberately it can help to strengthen the impression that the writer wants to make. Which sounds better: 'I came, I saw, I conquered' or 'I came, saw and conquered'?

Some words (such as 'get') are more common in speech than in writing. Others are often written but not usually found in conversation (for instance, 'nevertheless', or 'since' used in the sense of 'because'). A writer may use one of these words 'in the wrong place' to create a special effect; for example, to sound friendly, or to make one of his characters sound important or pompous.

Some words are rare, old-fashioned, or only found in certain contexts. (For instance, 'limpid', meaning 'clear', is mostly used in poetic descriptions.) And certain grammatical structures are old-fashioned or literary (putting the adjective after the noun, for example, or using 'that which' instead of 'what'). The use of words or structures like these can 'heighten' the style, and make the subject sound more important or romantic.

Comparisons are common in imaginative writing: they often have the effect of making an everyday object look new and different. (There are some good examples in the passage by Dylan Thomas in practice unit 9.1.)

A writer may also achieve an interesting effect by changing his style. Here is an amusing example from Oscar Wilde's story 'The Canterville Ghost' (about a ghost who meets another ghost):

'He chuckled to himself, and turned the corner; but no sooner had he done so, than, with a piteous wail of terror, he fell back, and hid his blanched face in his long, bony hands. Right in front of him was standing a horrible spectre, motionless as a carved image, and monstrous as a madman's dream! Its head was bald and burnished; its face round, and fat, and white; and hideous laughter seemed to have twisted its features into an eternal grin.

From the eyes streamed rays of scarlet light, the mouth was a wide well of fire, and a hideous garment, like his own, wrapped with its silent snows the Titan form. On its breast was a placard with strange writing in antique characters, some scroll of shame it seemed, some record of wild sins, some awful calendar of crime, and, with its right hand, it held a sword of gleaming steel.

Never having seen a ghost before, he naturally was terribly frightened.'

Humorous effects can often be achieved, as in this story, by using a particular style in an unexpected place. (People sometimes make a rather childish kind of joke by using a highly literary form of expression in ordinary conversation. For instance, somebody might say 'Let us partake of a little liquid refreshment as a preliminary to our repast' instead of 'Let's have a drink before lunch'.) Passages of humorous journalism are quite often set for comprehension tests in English examinations, so you should look out for this kind of thing.

Exercise a

Read the following passage slowly and carefully and then answer the questions.

Danny

This is the story of Danny and of Danny's friends and of Danny's house. It is a story of how these three became one thing, so that in Tortilla Flat if you speak of Danny's house you do not mean a structure of wood flaked with old white-wash, overgrown with an ancient untrimmed rose of Castile. No, when you speak of Danny's house you are understood to mean a unit of which the parts are men, from which came sweetness and joy, philan-   5
thropy and, in the end, a mystic sorrow. For Danny's house was not unlike the Round Table, and Danny's friends were not unlike the knights of it. And this is the story of how that group came into being, of how it flourished and grew to be an organization beautiful and wise. This story deals with the adventuring of Danny's friends, with the good they did, with their thoughts and their endeavors. In the end, this story tells how the   10
talisman was lost and how the group disintegrated.

From *Tortilla Flat* by John Steinbeck

1 Comment on the structure of the first sentence.
2 Why do you think the writer says 'if you speak of Danny's house' instead of 'if you talk about Danny's house'?
3 The 'Round Table' occurs in the heroic legends about King Arthur. Why is it referred to in this passage?
4 Comment on the expression 'an organization beautiful and wise'.
5 Why does the writer say 'their endeavors' instead of 'their efforts' or 'the things they tried to do'?
6 Comment on the way the sentences are constructed throughout the text.

Exercise b

Read the following passage slowly and carefully and then answer the questions.

The old man

He did not remember when he had first started to talk aloud when he was by himself.
He had sung when he was by himself in the old days and he had sung at night sometimes when he was alone steering on his watch in the smacks or in the turtle boats. He had
probably started to talk aloud, when alone, when the boy had left. But he did not
remember. When he and the boy fished together they usually spoke only when it was   5
necessary. They talked at night or when they were storm-bound by bad weather. It was
considered a virtue not to talk unnecessarily at sea and the old man had always considered
it so and respected it. But now he said his thoughts aloud many times since there was no
one that they could annoy.

'If the others heard me talking out loud they would think that I am crazy,' he said   10
aloud. 'But since I am not crazy, I do not care. And the rich have radios to talk to them in
their boats and to bring them the baseball.'

Now is no time to think of baseball, he thought. Now is the time to think of only one
thing. That which I was born for.

From *The Old Man and the Sea* by Ernest Hemingway

1 What does 'it' refer to in 'the old man had always considered it so' (lines 7–8)?
2 Comment on the grammar of the sentence beginning 'If the others heard me talking'.
3 Comment on the expression 'the rich have radios to talk to them'.
4 Comment on the sentence 'But since I am not crazy, I do not care'.
5 Comment on the expression 'That which I was born for'.
6 Why do you think the writer makes the old man talk in such an unnatural way?
7 There is a good deal of repetition in both of these passages. Does it seem to you to have
   the same effect in the two passages? What kind of words are repeated by Steinbeck and
   by Hemingway? What do you think is the purpose of each writer's use of repetition?

Practice unit 9.1

Read the text slowly and carefully and then answer the questions which follow.

Memories of childhood

There was another world where with my friends I used to dawdle on half-holidays
along the bent and Devon-facing sea-shore, hoping for gold watches or the skull of a
sheep or a message in a bottle to be washed up with the tide; and another where we used
to wander whistling through the packed streets, stale as station sandwiches, round the
impressive gas-works and the slaughter-house, past by the blackened monuments and   5
the museum that should have been in a museum. Or we scratched at a kind of cricket on
the bald and cindery surface of the recreation ground, or we took a tram that shook like
an iron jelly down to the gaunt pier*, there to clamber under the pier, hanging perilously
on to its skeleton legs or to run along to the end where patient men with the seaward
eyes of the dockside unemployed capped and muffled, dangling from their mouths   10
pipes that had long gone out, angled over the edge for unpleasant tasting fish.

Never was there such a town as ours, I thought, as we fought on the sand-hills with

* *pier*: a platform that sticks out into the sea

rough boys or dared each other to climb up the scaffolding of half-built houses soon to be called 'Laburnum' or 'The Beeches'. Never was there such a town, I thought, for the smell of fish and chips on Saturday evenings; for the Saturday afternoon cinema   15
matinées where we shouted and hissed our threepences away; for the crowds in the streets with leeks* in their hats on international nights*; for the park, the inexhaustible and mysterious, bushy Red-Indian hiding park where the hunchback sat alone and the groves* were blue with sailors. The memories of childhood have no order, and so I   19
remember that never was there such a dame school as ours, so firm and kind and smelling of galoshes, with the sweet and fumbled music of the piano lessons drifting down from upstairs to the lonely schoolroom, where only the sometimes tearful wicked sat over undone sums, or to repent a little crime – the pulling of a girl's hair during geography, the sly shin-kick under the table during English literature. Behind the school was a narrow lane where only the oldest and boldest threw pebbles at windows, scuffled   25
and boasted, fibbed about their relations:

> 'My father's got a chauffeur.'
> 'What's he want a chauffeur for, he hasn't got a car.'
> 'My father's the richest man in the town.'
> 'My father's the richest man in Wales.'   30
> 'My father owns the world.'

From 'Reminiscences of Childhood' by Dylan Thomas

Exercise

1 Comment on the expressions 'stale as station sandwiches' (line 4) and 'a tram that shook like an iron jelly' (lines 7–8).
2 Why does the writer say that the pier had 'skeleton legs' (line 9) instead of just 'thin legs'?
3 What does he mean by 'the museum that should have been in a museum' (line 6)?
4 What is meant by 'we scratched at a kind of cricket'?
5 What do you think is meant by the expression 'sea-ward eyes', and why does the writer use such an unusual word?
6 Explain 'we shouted and hissed our threepences away' (line 16).
7 Can you find some examples of poetic style in this passage?
8 What do you think is the writer's purpose?

Practice unit 9.2

Read the text slowly and carefully and then answer the questions that follow.

Puma humour

It was lunch-time in Harrow, London, and the locals were taking a quiet drink, reflecting peaceably about the greatness of Muhammad Ali and Mick Channon.

As the cigarette smoke wound idly towards the ceiling of the Tythe Farm Hotel, and beer mugs rose towards Harrovian lips, in walks this puma.

It was not an unaccompanied puma. Its owner, Mr John Goodman, had come for   5

---

* *leeks*: a leek is a vegetable, and also the national symbol of Wales
  international nights: the nights after international rugby football matches
  groves: groups of trees

a drink. The puma (the police described it as '12 months old, 3 ft. 6 in. long without tail, 2 ft. 6 in. high') had other ideas, and proceeded to rampage around a little. In the words of the police, it went berserk.

Tables were overturned, chairs flew about, and frightened customers headed for the alcoves, as the puma made the mistake of confusing the Tythe Farm Hotel with a small 10
jungle.

The police arrived and told Mr Goodman to restrain his puma. This proved difficult, but eventually Mr Goodman persuaded his puma to accompany him to his hired Morris Marina in the hotel car park. The puma got into the car – Mr Goodman did not. He closed the door, whereupon the puma mistook the inside of the Marina for an even 15
smaller jungle, and began some more rampaging. The upholstery did not survive the onslaught.

Harrow policemen are too sensible to open the Marina door before the puma has bolted, so they telephoned a local garage and arranged for car and contents to be towed to Harrow police station, the puma rampaging the while. Mr Goodman was also towed to 20
the police station, where he was charged with being drunk and incapable. He will appear in court this morning.

The puma, far from incapable and still rampaging in the Marina, now parked outside the police station, was not charged.

Instead the men who know about pumas, from London Zoo, were summoned to 25
cope with the large cat. They took it away to their zoo, where it now is, mixing it with feline friends but missing the warm atmosphere of the typical English pub.

An officer from Harrow police said: 'We treated the puma the same as we do all animals, the same as we do a dog. We like to do what is kindest for the animal.'

The charge against Mr Goodman, a packer who lives in Harrow, does not relate to the 30
puma. Scotland Yard said last night: 'As far as we know there's nothing illegal about keeping a puma. He acquired it legally from a breeder.'

As soon as news of a puma leaked about town, police thoughts, Harrovian thoughts, and journalistic thoughts, turned to that most famous of large cats, the 'Surrey puma,' reputed to be roaming the lanes of north Surrey during the late 'sixties. Many a courting 35
couple reported inconvenient interruptions as the creature suddenly appeared in the headlights.

But it was never caught, and it was never finally determined whether it was puma or myth. It made what with hindsight we can see as the fundamental mistake of not visiting pubs at lunchtime. 40

Report in *The Guardian*

Exercise

1 Why does the writer say 'in walks this puma' instead of 'in walked a puma'?
2 Comment on the style of the expression 'proceeded to rampage around a little'.
3 What does 'this', in line 12, refer to?
4 What effect does the writer want to create when he says 'the puma mistook the inside of the Marina for an even smaller jungle' (lines 15–16)?
5 Why does the writer say that Mr Goodman was 'towed' to the police station (line 20)?
6 Comment on the description of the puma as 'far from incapable' (line 23).
7 Comment on the phrase 'missing the warm atmosphere of the typical English pub' (line 27).
8 Compare the writer's treatment of his theme in the ninth and tenth paragraphs (lines 28–32) with his approach in the rest of the passage.

Practice unit 9.3

Read the three texts carefully and answer the questions which follow them.

First passage

Science and maths graduates

You could find your true reward in teaching.

   If you have a desire to help the younger generation, a wish to pass on your specialised knowledge, a way of communicating with youth, the ability to arouse the interest and curiosity of young minds; if you have patience, understanding, tact, a sense of responsibility and preferably a sense of humour, then to you, maths, science or engineering graduates, teaching could be the most rewarding and fulfilling career.   5

Advertisement in *The Times*

Exercise a

1 What is the purpose of this text?
2 Comment on the writer's choice of vocabulary.
3 Comment on the structure of the sentence beginning 'If you have a desire...'

Second passage

The great escape

Reserved for a lucky few.

   Those determined to put comfort before cost. And really get away from it all on the most exclusive holiday of its kind.

   A Royal Viking cruise.

   A rare opportunity of relaxing among a very select band of fellow voyagers. Instead of   5
being just one of a crowd.

   And a very different experience in cruising. Aboard the most impressive ships afloat.

   The three Royal Viking sister ships are designed purely for cruising the whole world over.
In superb style.

   They're all of Norwegian registry – and spirit.   10

   And all one class throughout – first.

   Which means a small, exclusive passenger complement on each. And a lot of distinct advantages.

   For a start, you'll more than likely enjoy a room with an ocean view (94% of our passengers do).   15

   You'll certainly have a splendid view from your dining table: both horizons at once. It can be almost as spectacular as the food at times.

   You'll also enjoy the leisurely comfort of meals at a single sitting (you're cruising first class, remember).

   Along with a standard of service that comes from having three crew members looking   20
after every five passengers.

   Right round the clock.

   Other pleasures abound, of course. Wide open teak decks. Big heated swimming pool.
Cinema and nightclub. Beauty Salon, saunas and shops.

Advertisement in *The Times*

Exercise b

1 What is the purpose of this text?
2 Compare briefly the sentence structure, vocabulary and style of this text with that of
the first text.

Third passage

What energy crisis?

There's plenty of petrol in the pumps. Lots of gas in the pipes. The home fires are burning,
and the lamps aren't going out all over Europe.

Funny sort of crisis. Which is probably why we're not doing enough about it.

But although we can't see it or feel it, the energy crisis is costing us a bomb.   4

In eighteen months, the price of crude oil (which provides almost half the energy we use)
has multiplied by five. And all our oil still has to be imported.

The bill we pay is £3,500,000,000 a year. Ten million pounds a day. A sum so big, it can't
possibly be your problem.

It is, though. That £10 million works out at 20p a day for every man, woman and child
in Britain. For a family of four, it's a millstone of £5.60 a week.   10

You can't shrug it off as a problem for the country to solve. Because the country is nothing
more than every man, woman and child in Britain.

Of course, in a few years, North Sea oil will help us pay our way. But we'll still have debts
to repay. And North Sea oil won't last forever.

We've simply got to Save It. Not just oil and petrol. But electricity, too, because oil   15
generates a quarter of it. And the less coal and gas we use, the more they're available to take
the place of oil.

What's more, we can save it without a lot of fuss and bother. Just with reasonable care.

Turn down a thermostat. Insulate a pipe. Clean out a furnace. Keep your car in tune.

You'll save a few pounds for yourself, and millions for Britain.   20

Advertisement in *The Observer*

Exercise c

1 What is the purpose of this text, and who is it directed at?
2 Comment on the way the arguments in the text are expressed.

Section D:
Practice tests

This section contains practice tests which are similar in form to those found in many English examinations. Time is often an important factor in examinations and suggested time-limits are given for each practice test.

Tests 1–4 are similar in style to the comprehension test in Cambridge Proficiency paper 1 section B; tests 5–8 are similar to paper 2 section B; tests 9–12 are similar to paper 3 section B. However, do not assume that the questions in your examination will have exactly the same form as these practice tests; examinations vary a little from year to year, and the number and type of passages and questions will not be quite the same each time.

Practice test 1

(Suggested time-limit: 1 hour)
Read the passage, and then answer the questions that follow it.

Conversation at breakfast

My mother shouted up the stairs: 'Billy? *Billy! Are* you getting up?' the third call in a fairly well-established series of street-cries that graduated from :'Are you awake, Billy?' to 'It's a quarter past nine, and you can stay in bed all day for all I care', meaning twenty to nine and time to get up. I waited until she called 'If I come up there you'll *know* about it' (a variant of number five, usually 'If I come up there I shall *tip* you out') and then I   5
got up.

I put on the old raincoat I used for a dressing-gown, and went downstairs. I was greeted by the usual breathing noises.

'You decided to get up, then,' my mother said, slipping easily into the second series of   9
conversations of the day. My stock replies were 'Yes', 'No, I'm still in bed', and a snarled 'What does it look like?' according to my mood. Today I chose 'Yes' and sat down to my boiled egg, stone cold as threatened. This made it a quarter to nine.

The old man looked up from some invoices and said: 'And you can start getting bloody well dressed before you come down in the morning.' So far the dialogue was taking a fairly conventional route and I was tempted to throw in one of the old stand-bys, 'Why do you always begin your sentences with an "And"?' Gran, another dress fanatic who always   16
seemed to be fully and even elaborately attired even at two in the morning when she slunk downstairs after the soda-water, chipped in: 'He wants to burn that raincoat, then he'll have to get dressed of a morning.' One of Gran's peculiarities, and she had many, was that she would never address anyone directly but always went through an intermediary,   20
if necessary some static object such as a cupboard. Doing the usual decoding I gathered that she was addressing my mother and that he who should burn the raincoat was the old

man, and he who would have to get dressed of a morning was me. 'I gather,' I began, 'that he who should burn the raincoat –' but the old man interrupted:

'And what bloody time did you get in last night? If you can call it last night. This 25 bloody morning, more like.'

From *Billy Liar* by Keith Waterhouse

1 Why does the writer use the word 'street-cries' (line 2)?
2 What have cry number five and its variant got in common?
3 Comment on the expression 'the usual breathing noises' (line 8).
4 '...slipping easily into the second series of conversations of the day' (lines 9–10). What was the first series?
5 What do you think 'stock replies' are (line 10)?
6 Why would Billy say 'No, I'm still in bed' (line 10)?
7 What is meant by 'This made it a quarter to nine' (line 12)?
8 What do you think 'one of the old stand-bys' means (line 15)?
9 Gran was 'another dress fanatic' (line 16). Who was the first?
10 Why does the writer say 'attired' instead of 'dressed' in line 17?
11 Gran speaks non-standard English. Can you give two examples from her sentence in lines 18–19 ('He wants to burn...')?
12 When, exactly, would Gran talk to a cupboard?
13 This passage shows how the conversation in a particular family reflects the unsatisfactory nature of their relationships. This is an important theme which can be dealt with in many different ways. Comment on the way this writer handles the subject.

Practice test 2

(Suggested time-limit: 1 hour)
Read the following passage and then answer the questions.

Twenty joke menthols, please

I suspect that I am not the only man who, every time he buys a packet of cigarettes, thinks of it, sometimes vaguely and sometimes quite resolutely, as the last one. I live permanently in the middle of a three-week period when things are a bit hectic; they've been a bit hectic for ten days, and I should have got through the worst of it in another ten days. Indeed by the time I have got through this very packet I shall be within sight of easier 5 times. I shall be on a calm, sunny plateau of my life. I shall hear again the vast, meaningful harmony of the universe. I shall become real, a holy content will suffuse me. I simply shan't *want* to smoke any more.

So it is quite a pleasant feeling, buying this last packet. It is like saying farewell to a schoolmaster, like buying an enormous meal on the quayside with one's last francs, like 10 shooting grouse on the last day of the season. Ah well, tobacco, you and I have been good friends...

In fact, I suffer from a mild delusion that I am giving up smoking all the time. And as with other and more violent delusions, long habituation has enabled me to live a perfectly happy, indeed a rather snug life with two perfectly opposite outlooks. In a way I can 15 quite see what it is like to think, with one part of one's mind, that one is a poached egg, while with another part one does things that one knows quite well no poached egg could

attempt, such as playing the piano or getting on a bus. And, just as there must be
sudden terrible moments when one stands right outside the whole thing, when one
realizes that this whole poached-egg business must cease, so do I experience sudden   20
cold blasts of reality about my non-smoking.

For instance, I have just been shaken by the extraordinary, the idiotic number and
variety of articles in the drawer where I keep all my non-smoking devices and subter-
fuges – things on which I have, for the last two years, been spending money *in addition*
to that spent on cigarettes. Somehow I had never noticed them as an aggregate,   25
a collection, before. It was really the addition to them, this week, of my latest failure,
a useless little cigarette-rolling machine, which somehow transformed this drawerful into
a significant and crazy museum collection. In this drawer, covered with dust, are the
following articles:

1. *The Three Expensive Pipes.* All failures. I tried all kinds of tobacco; light yellow   30
tobacco, and rich dark tobacco smelling of rum, out of cool jars in high-class, eighteenth-
century shops. Sometimes it would sizzle and drop red-hot pieces on to my writing pad.
Sometimes the smoke got into my eyes, since a pipe cannot be kept out of range, as it
were. There is nowhere you can put a pipe down for a second: it falls over on any ash-
tray. My pipes all filled up rapidly with coke and peat. I spent hours poking in them   35
with peculiar instruments, one of which is incised with the words

2. *Pipe Reamer*, and I see that in one of the distracted moments of the non-smoker
I have scratched another letter so that it now says Pipe Dreamer.

3. *The Great Bag of Herbs.* This is the remains of an ounce of some medical mixture I
once tried. It said in the advertisement it was good for asthma. I haven't got asthma,   40
so I reasoned it would be even better for me. It looks like dried lavender and pounded
bird's nests, and when first lit causes a thin crackling flame to rise from the pipe.
Other people in the room tend to like the gentle autumn melancholy of its garden-fire
smell; but it burns my tongue.

4. *The Green Tablets* (one after each meal) are supposed to make cigarettes taste awful.   45
But they make everything else, including my tongue, nay, my very soul, taste awful as
well. Also bad for the tongue is

5. *The Joke Menthol Cigarette* since the air hole in the celluloid thing holding the crystals
lets them escape into my mouth. I don't think one should *eat* menthol. The black
holder contains a rather childishly crude image of a half-burnt cigarette, with a sort of   50
tiny stage fire at the end, red paper and bright aluminium-powder ashes.

6. *The Cigarette Machine* makes even more extraordinary cigarettes than the ones
I tried to roll by hand. No two are the same. Some are convex, some are concave, like
a tiny pillow with all the stuffing pushed out of the middle; some are tapering. Some
burn half-way down the moment I light them, others are as solid as pencils and require   55
to be sucked until blue lights dance before my eyes, otherwise they go out. All have
loose ends, all come unstuck on my lips.

7. *Liquorice All-sorts, Lemon Sherbets, Barley Sugar, Curiously Strong Peppermints* like
all concentrated foods, induce a feeling of repletion and the desire to smoke.

In fact all these things, in their various ways, stimulate a desire for cigarettes. I must   60
cut down on them.

From *Model Oddlies* by Paul Jennings

1 Comment on the style of the three sentences beginning 'I shall be on a calm, sunny plateau' (lines 6–7).
2 What does 'it', in line 4, refer to?
3 Comment on the phrase 'buying this last packet' (line 9).
4 Why is this compared to 'saying farewell to a schoolmaster', etc.?
5 The sentence beginning 'Ah well, tobacco, you and I have been good friends' (lines 11–12) is unfinished. How could it have continued?
6 Explain the references in the third paragraph to a poached egg.
7 What is the purpose of the emphasis on 'in addition' (line 24)?
8 What does 'them', in line 25, refer to?
9 Comment on the use of the word 'non-smoker' in line 37.
10 Comment on the style of the sentence which begins 'Other people in the room...' (lines 43–4).
11 What does 'all', in line 56, refer to?
12 What do you think was the writer's main purpose in writing this passage?

Practice test 3

(Suggested time-limit: 1 hour)
Read the following text and then answer the questions which follow.

Lord Moping

'You will not find your father greatly changed,' remarked Lady Moping, as the car turned into the gates of the County Asylum.

'Will he be wearing a uniform?' asked Angela.

'No dear, of course not. He is receiving the very best attention.'

It was Angela's first visit and it was being made at her own suggestion. 5

Ten years had passed since the showery day in late summer when Lord Moping had been taken away; a day of confused but bitter memories for her; the day of Lady Moping's annual garden party, always bitter, confused that day by the caprice of the weather which, remaining clear and brilliant with promise until the arrival of the first guests, had suddenly blackened into a squall. There had been a scuttle for cover; the 10 marquee had capsized; a frantic carrying of cushions and chairs; a table-cloth lofted to the boughs of the monkey-puzzler, fluttering in the rain, a bright period and the cautious emergence of guests on to the soggy lawns; another squall; another twenty minutes of sunshine. It had been an abominable afternoon, culminating at about six o'clock in her father's attempted suicide. 15

Lord Moping habitually threatened suicide on the occasion of the garden party; that year he had been found black in the face, hanging by his braces in the orangery; some neighbours, who were sheltering there from the rain, set him on his feet again, and before dinner a van had called for him. Since then Lady Moping had paid seasonal calls at the asylum and returned in time for tea, rather reticent of her experience. 20

Many of her neighbours were inclined to be critical of Lord Moping's accommodation. He was not, of course, an ordinary inmate. He lived in a separate wing of the asylum, specially devoted to the segregation of wealthier lunatics. These were given every consideration which their foibles permitted. They might choose their own clothes (many

indulged in the liveliest fancies), smoke the most expensive brands of cigars and, on the   25
anniversaries of their certification, entertain any other inmates for whom they had an
attachment to private dinner parties.

    The fact remained, however, that it was far from being the most expensive kind of insti-
tution; the uncompromising address, 'COUNTY HOME FOR MENTAL DEFECTIVES',
stamped across the notepaper, worked on the uniforms of their attendants, painted, even,   30
upon a prominent hoarding at the main entrance, suggested the lowest associations. From
time to time, with less or more tact, her friends attempted to bring to Lady Moping's
notice particulars of seaside nursing homes, of 'qualified practitioners with large private
grounds suitable for the charge of nervous or difficult cases', but she accepted them
lightly; when her son came of age he might make any changes that he thought fit; mean-   35
while she felt no inclination to relax her economical régime; her husband had betrayed
her basely on the one day in the year when she looked for loyal support, and was far better
off than he deserved.

From *Mr Loveday's Little Outing* by Evelyn Waugh

1   Comment on Lady Moping's way of speaking (lines 1–4).
2   The paragraph beginning 'Ten years had passed' (lines 6–15) is written in a rather
     different style from the rest of the passage. What do you think is the reason for this?
3   Comment on the use of the expression 'of course' in lines 4 and 22.
4   Who or what are 'these' in line 23?
5   What does the word 'it', in line 28, refer to?
6   What is meant by the expression 'the uncompromising address' in line 29?
7   Explain 'suggested the lowest associations' (line 31).
8   Compare the language of the two expressions 'COUNTY HOME FOR MENTAL
     DEFECTIVES' (line 29) and 'qualified practitioners with large private grounds suitable
     for the charge of nervous or difficult cases' (lines 33–4).
9   Why exactly did Lady Moping feel that her husband 'had betrayed her basely' (lines
     36–7)?

Practice test 4

(Suggested time-limit: 1 hour)
Read the following text and then answer the questions.

At these prices, who can afford not to?

If shoplifting food seems easy, it's nothing compared to the snatching of clothing. Shop
only the better stores. Try things on in those neat little secluded stalls, the less bulky
items, such as shirts, vests, belts and socks can be tied around your waist or leg with large
rubber bands if needed. Just take a number of items in and come out with a few less.

    In some cities there are still free stores left over from the flower power days. Churches   5
often have give-away clothing programs. You can impersonate a clergyman and call
one of the large clothing manufacturers in your area. They are usually willing to donate
a case or two of shirts, trousers or underwear to your church raffle or drive to dress up
skid row. Be sure to get your sizes. Tell them 'your boy' will pick up the blessed donation
and you'll mention his company in the evening prayers.   10

If you notice people moving from an apartment or house, ask them if they'll be leaving behind clothing. They usually abandon all sorts of items including food, furniture and books. Offer to help them carry out stuff if you can keep what they won't be taking.

Make the rounds of a fancy neighborhood with a truck and some friends. Ring doorbells and tell the person who answers that you are collecting wearable clothing for 15 the 'poor homeless victims of the recent tidal wave in Quianto, a small village in Saudi Arabia.' You get the pitch. Make it food and clothing, and say you're with a group called Heartline for Decency. A phony letter from a church might help here.

Notice if your friends have lost or gained weight. A big change means a lot of clothes doing nothing but taking up closet space. Show up at dormitories when college is over 20 for the summer and winter season. Go to the train or bus stations and tell them you left your raincoat, gloves or umbrella when you came into town. They'll take you to a room with thousands of unclaimed items. Pick out what you like. While there, notice a neat suitcase or trunk and memorize the markings. Later a friend can claim the item. There will be loads of surprises in any suitcase. We have a close friend who inherited ten kilos 25 of grass* this way.

Apartment lobbies are good for all kinds of neat furniture. If you want to get fancy about it, rent a truck (not one that says U-HAUL-IT or other rental markings) and make the pick-up with moving-man type uniforms. When schools are on strike and students hold seminars and debate into the night, Yippies can be found going through the dorm 30 lobbies and storage closets hauling off couches, desks, printing supplies, typewriters, mimeos, etc. to store in secret underground nests. A nervy group of Yippies in the Midwest tried to swipe a giant IBM 360 computer while a school was in turmoil. All power to those that bring a wheelbarrow to sit-ins.

Check into a high-class hotel or motel remembering to dress like the wallpaper. 35 Carry a large dummy suitcase with you and register under a phony name. Make sure you and not the bellboy carry this bag. Use others as a decoy. When you get inside the room, grab everything you can stuff in the suitcase: radio, TV sets (even if it has a special plug you can cut it with a knife and remove the cord), blankets, toilet paper, glasses, towels, sheets, lamps (forget the imitation Winslow Homer on the wall), a Bible, soap, and toss 40 rugs. Before you leave (odd hours are best) hang the DO NOT DISTURB sign on the doorknob; this will give you an extra few hours to beat it across the border or check into a new hotel.

Landlords renovating buildings throw out stoves, tables, lamps, refrigerators and carpeting. In most cities, each area has a day designated for discarding bulk objects. Call 45 the Sanitation Department and say you live in that part of town which would be putting out the most expensive shit and find out the pick-up day. Fantastic buys can be found cruising streets late at night. Check out the backs of large department stores for floor models, window displays and slightly damaged furniture being discarded.

From *Steal this Book* by Abbie Hoffman

1 Comment on the expression 'these prices' in the title of the passage.
2 'Just take a number of items in and come out with a few less' (line 4). What happens to the other items?
3 Comment on the language of the expression 'the blessed donation' in line 9.
4 What is meant by 'it' in 'make it food and clothing' (line 17)?
5 Who are 'they' in line 22?

* *grass*: marihuana (slang)

6 What does 'this way' (line 26) refer to?
7 The word 'neat' (lines 2, 23, 27) is American slang. What do you think it means?
8 Comment on the author's choice of language in the expression 'dress like the wallpaper' (line 35).
9 Comment briefly (1–2 sentences) on the author's choice of vocabulary and grammatical constructions.
10 What do you think is the main purpose of the passage?

Practice test 5

(Suggested time-limit: 50 minutes)
In this test you will find after each of the passages a number of questions or unfinished statements about the passage, each with four suggested answers. Write down the numbers of the questions, followed by the letters corresponding to the most appropriate answers. Give one answer only to each question. Read each passage right through before choosing your answers.

First passage

Left holding the baby

Scientists recently revealed an instinct in women intact and unaffected by the age of technology. Glancing through glossy art books Lee Salk (*Scientific American*, May 1973) noticed that four times out of five Mary is depicted holding the infant Jesus against her left breast. The Madonna sparked off a series of experiments and observations to determine on which side women hold their babies and why. 5

First he determined that modern mothers still tend to hold their baby on the left. Of 255 right-handed mothers, 83% held the baby on the left. And out of 32 left-handed women, 78% held the baby on the left. As a control, women were watched emerging from supermarkets carrying baby-sized packages; the bundles were held with no side preference. 10

Then, dental patients were given a large rubber ball to hold during treatment. The majority clutched the ball to their left side, even when it interfered with the dentist's activities. This suggested that in times of stress objects are held against the left side.

At that point an apparently contradictory phenomenon was observed. A large number of mothers who brought their premature babies to a follow-up clinic were seen to hold 15 their babies against their right side.

So, 115 mothers who had been separated from their babies for 24 hours after birth were observed for holding response. The experimenters presented the baby directly to the mid-line of the mother's body, and noted how she held the baby. 53% placed the baby on the left and 47% on the right. And it was also noted that the mothers of the group who had 20 held their baby on the left had already had a baby from which they had not been separated after birth.

The author suggests that 'the time immediately after birth is a critical period when the stimulus of holding the baby releases a certain maternal response.' That is to say, she senses the baby is better off on her left. 25

Left-handed holding enables the baby to hear the heartbeat – a sound associated with the security of the womb. In order to discover whether hearing the heart has a beneficial effect on the baby, the sound of a human heartbeat was played to 102 babies in a New York nursery for 4 days. A control group of babies was not exposed to heartbeats. The babies in the beat group gained markedly more weight and cried far less than the babies in the control group.

30

From an article in *Spare Rib*

1 Looking at art books inspired Lee Salk to investigate
a) pictures of Mary and Jesus.
b) the way mothers hold their babies.
c) the way people hold objects in times of stress.
d) the effect of the human heartbeat on premature babies.

2 He found that
a) left-handed women tend to hold their babies on the right.
b) only right-handed women tend to hold their babies on the left.
c) more right-handed women than left-handed women tend to hold their babies on the left.
d) women who hold their babies on the left are nearly all right-handed.

3 Why did he watch women coming out of supermarkets?
a) to control them
b) to see how they carried their babies
c) to see if women carried parcels and babies differently
d) to see if the women were right-handed or left-handed

4 Why were dental patients given a rubber ball to hold?
a) to help them overcome their stress
b) to help the dentist's activity
c) because of the experiment
d) to see which side they held it on

5 The word 'this' (line 13) refers to
a) a large rubber ball (line 11)
b) the majority (line 12)
c) the fact that the ball interfered with the dentist's activity
d) the fact that the patients held the ball on the left

6 What was the 'apparently contradictory phenomenon' (line 14)?
a) Mothers of premature babies were seen to hold their children differently from other mothers.
b) Mothers of premature babies held their babies on the correct side.
c) Mothers of premature babies took their babies to a follow-up clinic.
d) The behaviour of mothers of premature babies disproved Lee Salk's theory.

7 Mothers were observed 'for holding response' (line 18). This means:
a) to see how they answered experimenters' questions
b) to see how they held their babies
c) to see how they spoke to their babies
d) to test their reaction to separation from their babies

8 The time just after birth is important: this is when
a) babies must not be separated from their mothers.
b) the baby's response to the mother is released.
c) the mother has an instinctive tendency to hold the baby on the left.
d) the baby can hear the mother's heartbeat.

9 In one experiment, 102 babies spent four days
a) not exposed to heartbeats.
b) in a control group.
c) exposed to the sound of heartbeats.
d) in a New York beat group.

10 Salk's experiments proved that
a) mothers have an instinct to hold their babies on the left immediately after birth.
b) mothers hold their babies on the left at times of stress.
c) mothers of premature babies do not have the instinct to hold their babies on the left.
d) mothers find it more comfortable to carry their babies on the left because the heart is on that side.

Second passage

Submarine rescue

Two men trapped in a midget submarine more than 200 feet down on the bed of the North Sea returned safely to the surface last night. They were rescued by two free-swimming divers who after a 20-minute struggle in the darkness, cut through the rope that had fouled their vessel's propeller.

The submarine , which had become trapped while working near a Shell oil produc-   5
tion rig at about 1.30 p.m., rose to the surface on its own and by 7 p.m. the crew were aboard their mother ship 'for a rest, feeling fine.'

The rescue went smoothly because the position of the trapped submersible was known quite accurately and the depth – variously reported to be between 200 and 275 feet – was only moderate by modern diving standards. In addition support vessels   10
with divers and equipment were on hand, and the weather was unusually calm. But the thoughts of those involved will have gone back to the much more serious emergency involving the Pisces III last year in the Atlantic, and there is bound to be a renewed call – from MPs if not from the diving firms – for the tighter safety rules which were discussed then.   15

Mr John Prescott, the MP for Hull East, said last night that he would like to see emergency procedures similar to those used by the Royal Navy. He intended to raise the idea of a marine authority that would co-ordinate rescue operations of this kind. The new Merchant Shipping Act, passed by the last Parliament, did lay down pro-visions for submarine operations, but it only applied to British ships.   20

The men trapped yesterday were both Americans, Gilbert Blevins and Leslie Lynch from Louisiana. They were working from the mother ship *William Dampier* on Shell's Auk oilfield about 180 miles NE of Dundee. Shell is establishing a production rig on the seabed there and nearby is a mooring buoy to which ships can attach themselves. This in turn has a number of anchors laid out on the bottom, but one of these was found to   25
be out of position.

The job of the TS1 submersible was to take down a half-inch circumference poly-
propylene line and, using remote controlled mechanical arms, pass this through a fitting
on the anchor – probably a shackle – so that a heavy lifting cable could later be fed
down. With the line already threaded through, it seems, and tending to float to the
surface, it got caught in the submarine's propeller and wrapped round the shaft.

It is a situation with which every weekend yachtsman is familiar, but at a depth of
more than 200 feet – from which a free ascent by the crew would have been difficult
and dangerous – it could have been fatal. The TS1, a 26-foot American submersible,
which does not have a 'lock out' chamber through which divers can come and go, had
40 hours of air supply for the crew. Had the propeller been more seriously fouled, by
chain for example, the rescue divers might have worked first to connect an air line from
the mother ship on the surface. In fact, they went down in a diving bell, swam out,
cut through the line and unravelled it.

The key to the success of the operation, given that divers capable of working at
those depths happened to be available on the pipe-laying barge *Challenger* in the first place,
was the comparative ease with which they could pin down the submarine's position.
If necessary, they could probably have followed the cable down from the buoy to the
anchor.

From *The Guardian*

1 The two trapped men
a) were released from their submarine by two divers.
b) managed to free the submarine's propeller.
c) rose to the surface in their submarine.
d) were resting on the surface in their submarine at 7 p.m.

2 The submarine was trapped because
a) the engines failed.
b) rope pulled the propeller off.
c) it got stuck in the mud.
d) rope got caught round the propeller.

3 How many reasons does the writer give for the success of the rescue?
a) one
b) two
c) three
d) four

4 The writer suggests that the incident will make people
a) ask for stricter safety regulations.
b) ask for safety regulations for the Royal Navy.
c) ask for a new Merchant Shipping Act.
d) ask for tighter regulations for British ships.

5 'Lay down provisions' (lines 19–20) means
a) make rules
b) put anchors on the seabed
c) provide supplies
d) ease the regulations

6 The general purpose of the work in the North Sea described in the article is
a) getting oil from the seabed.
b) underwater exploration.
c) establishing a mooring buoy.
d) laying anchors on the seabed.

7 The submarine went down
a) to move an anchor.
b) to take down a rope half an inch long.
c) to pull the anchor into position with mechanical arms.
d) to put a thin rope through part of the anchor.

8 'It' (line 34) refers to
a) the anchor.
b) the fact that the anchor was out of position.
c) the fact that the submarine's propeller had rope round it.
d) the fact that the submarine was too deep for safety.

9 The rescue was possible mainly
a) because of improved modern diving methods.
b) because they had enough air.
c) because the rescuers knew exactly where the submarine was.
d) because it was a modern American submarine.

10 The main subject of the passage is
a) safety regulations for submarines.
b) a submarine rescue.
c) diving methods.
d) oil from the sea.

Practice test 6

(Suggested time-limit: 50 minutes)
In this test you will find after each of the passages a number of questions or unfinished statements about the passage, each with four suggested answers. Write down the numbers of the questions, followed by the letters corresponding to the most appropriate answers. Give one answer only to each question. Read each passage right through before choosing your answers.

First passage

Perception

It is often helpful when thinking about biological processes to consider some apparently similar yet better understood *non*-biological process. In the case of visual perception an obvious choice would be colour photography. Since in many respects eyes resemble cameras, and percepts photographs, is it not reasonable to assume that perception is a sort of photographic process whereby samples of the external world become spontaneously and accurately reproduced somewhere inside our heads? Unfortunately, the answer must be no. The best that can be said of the photographic analogy is that it points up what perception is not. Beyond this it is superficial and misleading. Four simple experiments should make the matter plain. 5

In the first a person is asked to match a pair of black and white discs, which are 10
rotating at such a speed as to make them appear uniformly grey. One disc is standing in
shadow, the other in bright illumination. By adjusting the ratio of black to white in
one of the discs the subject tries to make it look the same as the other. The results show him
to be remarkably accurate, for it seems he has made the proportion of black to white
in the brightly illuminated disc almost identical with that in the disc which stood in 15
shadow. But there is nothing photographic about his perception, for when the matched
discs, still spinning, are photographed, the resulting print shows them to be quite
dissimilar in appearance. The disc in shadow is obviously very much darker than the
other one. What has happened? Both the camera and the person were accurate, but their
criteria differed. One might say that the camera recorded things as they look, and the 20
person things as they are. But the situation is manifestly more complex than this, for the
person also recorded things as they look. He did better than the camera because he
made them look as they really are. He was not misled by the differences in illumination.
He showed perceptual constancy. By reason of an extremely rapid, wholly unconscious
piece of computation he received a more accurate record of the external world than 25
could the camera.

In the second experiment a person is asked to match with a colour card the colours of
two pictures in dim illumination. One is of a leaf, the other of a donkey. Both are coloured
an equal shade of green. In making his match he chooses a much stronger green for the
leaf than for the donkey. The leaf evidently looks greener than the donkey. The 30
percipient makes a perceptual world compatible with his own experience. It hardly needs
saying that cameras lack this versatility.

In the third experiment hungry, thirsty and satiated people are asked to equalize
the brightness of pictures depicting food, water and other objects unrelated to hunger
or thirst. When the intensities at which they set the pictures are measured it is found 35
that hungry people see pictures relating to food as brighter than the rest (i.e. to
equalize the pictures they make the food ones less intense), and thirsty people do like-
wise with 'drink' pictures. For the satiated group no differences are obtained between
the different objects. In other words, perception serves to satisfy needs, not to enrich
subjective experience. Unlike a photograph the percept is determined by more than 40
just the stimulus.

The fourth experiment is of a rather different kind. With ears plugged, their eyes
beneath translucent goggles and their bodies either encased in cotton wool, or floating
naked in water at body temperature, people are deprived for considerable periods of
external stimulation. Contrary to what one might expect, however, such circum- 45
stances result not in a lack of perceptual experience but rather a surprising change in
what is perceived. The subjects in such an experiment begin to see, feel and hear things
which bear no more relationship to the immediate external world than does a dream
in someone who is asleep. These people are not asleep yet their hallucinations, or so-
called 'autistic' perceptions, may be as vivid, if not more so, than any normal percept. 50

From 'The beginnings of perception' by N. F. Dixon

1   In the first paragraph, the author suggests that
a) colour photography is a biological process.
b) vision is rather like colour photography.
c) vision is a sort of photographic process.
d) vision and colour photography are very different.

2   The word 'it', in line 8, refers to
a) perception.
b) the photographic process.
c) the comparison with photography.
d) the answer.

3   In the first experiment, it is proved that a person
a) makes mistakes of perception and is less accurate than a camera.
b) can see more clearly than a camera.
c) is more sensitive to changes in light than a camera.
d) sees colours as they are in spite of changes in the light.

4   The word 'that', in line 15, refers to
a) the proportion of black to white.
b) the brightly illuminated disc.
c) the other disc.
d) the grey colour.

5   The second experiment shows that
a) people see colours according to their ideas of how things should look.
b) colours look different in a dim light.
c) cameras work less efficiently in a dim light.
d) colours are less intense in larger objects.

6   'Satiated', in line 33, means
a) tired
b) bored
c) not hungry or thirsty
d) nervous

7   What does 'to equalize the brightness' (lines 33–4) mean?
a) To arrange the pictures so that the equally bright ones are together.
b) To change the lighting so that the pictures look equally bright.
c) To describe the brightness.
d) To move the pictures nearer or further away.

8   The third experiment proves that
a) we see things differently according to our interest in them.
b) pictures of food and drink are especially interesting to everybody.
c) cameras are not good at equalising brightness.
d) satiated people see less clearly than hungry or thirsty people.

9   The expression 'contrary to what one might expect' occurs in line 45. What might one expect?
a) that the subjects would go to sleep
b) that they would feel uncomfortable and disturbed
c) that they would see, hear and feel nothing
d) that they would see, hear and feel strange things

10 The fourth experiment proves
a) that people deprived of sense stimulation go mad.
b) that people deprived of sense stimulation dream.
c) that people deprived of sense stimulation experience unreal things.
d) that people deprived of sense stimulation lack perceptual experience.

11 The group of experiments, taken together, prove that human perception is
a) unreliable.
b) mysterious and unpredictable.
c) less accurate than a camera.
d) related to our knowledge, experience and needs.

Second passage

Margo and Peter

As the summer drew to a close I found myself, to my delight, once more without
a tutor. Mother had discovered that, as she so delicately put it, Margo and Peter were
becoming 'too fond of one another'. As the family was unanimous in its disapproval of
Peter as a prospective relation by marriage, something obviously had to be done.
Leslie's only contribution to the problem was to suggest shooting Peter, a plan that   5
was, for some reason, greeted derisively. I thought it was a splendid idea, but I was in
the minority. Larry's suggestion that the happy couple should be sent to live in Athens
for a month, in order, as he explained, to get it out of their systems, was quashed by
Mother on the grounds of immorality. Eventually Mother dispensed with Peter's services,
he left hurriedly and furtively and we had to cope with a tragic, tearful and wildly   10
indignant Margo, who, dressed in her most flowing and gloomy clothing for the event,
played her part magnificently. Mother soothed and uttered gentle platitudes, Larry gave
Margo lectures on free love, and Leslie, for reasons best known to himself, decided
to play the part of the outraged brother and kept appearing at intervals, brandishing
a revolver and threatening to shoot Peter down like a dog if he set foot in the house   15
again. In the midst of all this Margo, tears trickling effectively down her face, made
tragic gestures and told us her life was blighted. Spiro, who loved a good dramatic
situation as well as anyone, spent his time weeping in sympathy with Margo, and
posting various friends of his along the docks to make sure that Peter did not attempt to
get back on to the island. We all enjoyed ourselves very much. Just as the thing   20
seemed to be dying a natural death, and Margo was able to eat a whole meal without
bursting into tears, she got a note from Peter saying he would return for her. Margo,
rather panic-stricken by the idea, showed the note to Mother, and once more the
family leapt with enthusiasm into the farce. Spiro doubled his guard on the docks,
Leslie oiled his guns and practised on a large cardboard figure pinned to the front of   25
the house, Larry went about alternately urging Margo to disguise herself as a peasant
and fly to Peter's arms, or to stop behaving like Camille. Margo, insulted, locked herself
in the attic and refused to see anyone except me, as I was the only member of the family
who had not taken sides. She lay there, weeping copiously, and reading a volume of
Tennyson; occasionally she would break off to consume a large meal – which   30
I carried up on a tray – with undiminished appetite.

From *My Family and Other Animals* by Gerald Durrell

1 What is meant by 'the family was unanimous in its disapproval of Peter as a pros-
    pective relation by marriage' (lines 3–4)?
a) They did not like him.
b) They did not want him to marry Margo.
c) They all had different attitudes to him.
d) They expressed their disapproval loudly.

2 'For some reason', in line 6, means
a) for several reasons
b) for a good reason
c) for an unknown reason
d) for the reason that follows

3 Larry suggested sending Margo and Peter to Athens so that
a) they could get away from the family.
b) they could get away from ordinary society.
c) they would get tired of living together.
d) they would get used to married life in Athens.

4 'In the midst of all this' (line 16) – 'all this' means
a) Leslie's threats
b) Margo's sorrow
c) Margo's dramatisation of the situation
d) everything that was going on

5 Spiro seemed to be
a) on Margo's side.
b) on the family's side.
c) on both sides.
d) determined to make a joke of the whole affair.

6 What was the family's main reaction to Margo's distress?
a) They offered useless advice and suggestions.
b) They laughed at her.
c) They were sympathetic.
d) They quarrelled about it.

7 What attitude did Margo's family take towards Peter?
a) They all had the same attitude except Larry.
b) They all had the same attitude except the narrator.
c) They all had the same attitude.
d) They all had different attitudes.

8 During the whole episode, the family
a) showed that they appreciated the tragic side of it.
b) were very cruel to Margo.
c) deliberately tried to make Margo laugh.
d) behaved as if they were acting in a play.

9 How did Margo's state of mind change during the affair?
a) First she was panic-stricken, then indifferent.
b) First she was unhappy, then frightened, then angry.
c) At first her feelings were genuine, but later she dramatised them.
d) At first she was against everybody, but later she became more friendly to the narrator.

Practice test 7

(Suggested time-limit: 50 minutes)
In this test you will find after each of the passages a number of questions or unfinished
statements about the passage, each with four suggested answers. Write down the numbers

of the questions, followed by the letters corresponding to the most appropriate answers. Give one answer only to each question. Read each passage right through before choosing your answers.

First passage

Gentle ghost

For the past month there have been a couple of Glaswegian ex-thugs (their description) patching up our house. They arrive, unpredictably, any time between 10.30 a.m. and 2 p.m. to start work. They've consumed most of the coffee in the house and finished our precious sugar and they don't have an ounce of official jargon between them. What they have done is a job which knocks spots off the efforts of the 'official' builders   5 we employed earlier in the year, at far less cost and with that rare attribute, enthusiasm.

We found these two through Gentle Ghost, a community organisation based in a brightly coloured house at the back of Notting Hill Gate, which operates an employment agency aiming to bring some level of ideology to the work situation as well as supplying almost anything you might want from an astrologer to removal man,   10 loo cleaner to film director.

Hugh Berger, a well-preened ex-Harrovian, started Gentle Ghost ('I wanted the name to sound sort of spiritual') four and a half years ago with the idea of providing a 'happy, dignified working structure which would be better for both workers and clients.' He explains that our society forces everyone into restrictive working roles with   15 too little responsibility for themselves, and virtually no freedom to step outside the imposed idea of a five-day week.

He got together with a group of people who wanted to work part-time, on their own terms, placed an ad. in *Time Out* and sat for several weeks by the telephone in his flat liaising between his 'team' and callers wanting odd jobs done.   20

From there the team grew, so that now they have university graduates, social service workers, teachers, journalists, film-makers, photographers as well as plumbers, carpenters, builders and a fleet of people who do removals on their books. The age range is 20–60, and they handle 30–40 jobs a day.

As Gentle Ghost was set up as an alternative to a society worshipping money more   25 than dignity, Hugh Berger was determined that fees should be kept low and to help this the agency takes only a 15 per cent commission from workers, to cover (just about) their overheads. Accordingly most of the work they do is considerably cheaper than quotes from the traditional agencies.

'This is an important part of our people taking responsibility for themselves: if they   30 feel a client is very hard up and want to drop their fee or do a job for free that's fine. We would never complain,' Hugh Berger says.

Anyone joining Gentle Ghost's books undergoes a couple of stiff interviews and is weeded out, if he or she doesn't prove up to scratch 'although it's a painful process as the Ghost house acts as a community centre and we get to know and like almost everyone,'   35 says Hugh Berger. But still, there are problems. One woman liked her worker and paid him before he finished the job, then he vanished. Gentle Ghost admits this can happen, but they insist it's unusual and if it does they guarantee to get someone else to finish the job as cheaply as possible and hopefully for nothing.

Since it began, Gentle Ghost has broadened its scope and now holds evening classes   40 in such things as yoga, astrology, massage, hypnotherapy, creative drama and skills such

as plumbing and carpentry. They also have an open restaurant at nearly cost prices and
a help and advice centre for anyone in need.

'They tend to complement one another,' Hugh Berger explains, 'because if someone's
in a bad state and needs to work we try to help by sending him out with a responsible   45
worker until he's fit to go alone, and if people are lonely they can sit around in the
restaurant, come to our evening classes or encounter groups and get involved with the
life of Ghost.

'The group of us who run Ghost form a nucleus but the people working with us are
every bit as important and what we have done is to build up a really caring com-   50
munity which functions as an alternative within society.

'I would love to see other people setting up similar organisations and I am here to give
advice to anyone who wants it. If people would just stop moaning about their bosses
and go out on a limb, probably everyone would be happier,' is the conviction with
which Hugh Berger rounded off our talk.   55

Report in *The Guardian* by Angela Neustatter

1   The two Glaswegians are
a) less reliable than the 'official' builders.
b) as good as the 'official' builders.
c) more ideological than the ' official ' builders.
d) more efficient than the 'official' builders.

2   They do not start work at the same time every day because
a) Gentle Ghost's staff have more freedom than most workers.
b) it suits the clients.
c) it is difficult to get staff who will work regular hours.
d) they are ex-thugs.

3   Their work costs less than the 'official' builders' job because
a) they are enthusiastic.
b) Gentle Ghost use unqualified workmen.
c) Gentle Ghost have a policy of not making large profits.
d) Gentle Ghost have lower overheads than most firms.

4   Gentle Ghost is basically
a) a builders' community.
b) a small business which also runs evening classes.
c) a combination of a community and an employment agency.
d) an organisation which wishes to revolutionise society.

5   The phrase 'to bring some level of ideology to the work situation' (line 9) means
a) to make people think about their work
b) to give work more meaning
c) to bring politics into work
d) to make work more efficient

6   What is 'a society worshipping money more than dignity' (lines 25–6)?
a) another employment agency
b) the organisation Berger worked for before
c) a way of describing the attitude of Gentle Ghost's customers
d) the society most of us live in

7 What is meant by 'to cover their overheads' (lines 27–8)?
a) to keep a roof over their heads
b) to pay their expenses
c) to pay the tax bill
d) to take care of unexpected extra expenses

8 'Up to scratch', in line 34, means
a) good enough
b) revolutionary enough
c) normal
d) honest

9 'Broadened its scope' (line 40) means
a) become more successful
b) changed its attitude
c) taken on more activities
d) moved into bigger premises

10 The restaurant and the help and advice centre are for
a) the staff of Gentle Ghost only.
b) the community.
c) anyone who needs them.
d) the nucleus of Gentle Ghost.

11 The purpose of Gentle Ghost is
a) to provide employment for its staff.
b) to provide cheap services and labour for the public in Notting Hill.
c) to help people who are in a bad state.
d) to provide an acceptable working and living situation for its members.

Second passage

Ski-ing down Everest

Katmandu, May 17

Mr Yuichiro Miura, the Japanese skier, told reporters in Katmandu today how he
narrowly escaped death in his attempt to ski down Mount Everest earlier this month.

His descent began at 25,918 ft above sea level and ended when he fell 100 yards
short of a crevasse, he said. In the final seconds, as he hurtled down the mountainside
at about 50 miles an hour, dodging boulders in his path, he was convinced that he   5
was about to be killed. The fall saved his life.

Mr Miura's 1·8 mile ski run on May 6 was elaborately organized. He first climbed
820 ft above the starting point for an easy 30-second run down to the South Col in normal
alpine ski-ing conditions on excellent snow. Within a few hours, after spending more than
90 minutes checking his equipment, he began the fast descent.   10

He said that he began the downhill run as soon as winds decreased and within
five seconds he was rushing headlong at 100 miles an hour. The 40-degree slope soon
narrowed abruptly, with exposed rocks on either side, and the winds buffeted him from
both sides.

He found that at times his brake parachute was failing to slow his descent, and he   15
tried to check his speed by pressing the edges of his skis harder into the snow.

A minute later he found that he was ski-ing over undulating rock-strewn ice. He hit one of the boulders at an altitude of about 23,600 ft, went out of control, slithered, lost his right ski and crashed into a boulder. Almost unconscious, he finally came to a halt close to the crevasse. But he was unhurt.

20

From *The Times*

1 Why did Mr Miura's fall save his life?
a) Because he did not fall too hard.
b) Because otherwise he would have been killed by crashing into a boulder.
c) Because it stopped his attempt to ski down Everest.
d) Because if he had not fallen he would not have been able to avoid going into a crevasse.

2 He climbed 820 feet
a) and then did a short practice run.
b) and then started the descent of Everest.
c) and started his descent 30 seconds later.
d) and went down to the South Col a few hours later.

3 'Checking his equipment' (line 10) means
a) putting on his equipment
b) making sure his equipment was all right
c) collecting his equipment
d) cleaning his equipment

4 'The 40-degree slope soon narrowed abruptly' (lines 12-13). This means
a) it suddenly got steeper
b) Miura suddenly had less room on either side
c) it got much rougher suddenly
d) it got less steep suddenly

5 'With exposed rocks on either side' (line 13) means
a) rocks stuck out of the snow all around him
b) rocks stuck out of the snow first on one side, then on the other
c) rocks stuck out of the snow on both sides
d) there were cliffs on both sides

6 Miura was unable to slow down
a) because of the rocks.
b) because the edges of his skis weren't working properly.
c) because of the wind.
d) because he was going too fast and part of his equipment wasn't working properly.

7 'To check his speed' (line 16) means
a) to stop
b) to calculate his speed
c) to slow down
d) to turn

8 He finally lost control
a) because he hit a boulder.
b) because he was ski-ing on ice.
c) because the ice was undulating.
d) because he lost a ski.

9   Miura's attempt to ski down Everest
a) was successful despite the difficulties.
b) failed because of problems he had not expected.
c) failed although it had been perfectly prepared.
d) was almost successful despite the difficulties.

Practice test 8

(Suggested time-limit: 50 minutes)
In this test you will find after each of the passages a number of questions or unfinished
statements about the passage, each with four suggested answers. Write down the numbers
of the questions, followed by the numbers corresponding to the most appropriate
answers. Give one answer only to each question. Read each passage right through before
choosing your answers.

First passage

Home-made atomic bomb

Tomorrow evening about 20 million Americans will be shown, on their television screens,
how easy it is to steal plutonium and produce 'the most terrifying blackmail weapon
ever devised' – a home-made atomic bomb.

They will be told that no commercial nuclear plant in the United States – and probably
in the world – is adequately protected against a well planned armed attack by terrorists,   5
and that there is enough information on public record to guide a nuclear thief not only
to the vaults of nuclear plants where plutonium is stored, but also to tell him how the doors
of those vaults are designed.

The hour-long television programme, 'The Plutonium Connection', makes its point
by showing how a 20-year-old student of the Massachusetts Institute of Technology in   10
five weeks designed an atomic bomb composed of plutonium and parts from a hardware
store.

The young man, whose identity is being kept secret for fear he may be kidnapped
by terrorists, is quoted as saying: 'I was pretty surprised about how easy it is to design
a bomb. When I was working on my design, I kept thinking there's got to be more to it   15
than this, but actually there isn't. It's simple.'

The student worked alone, using information he obtained from science libraries open
to the public. The television programme, produced for non-commercial stations across
the country by a Boston educational station, shows how quantities of other 'secret'
information are available to anyone.   20

The Atomic Energy Commission's public reading room in Washington is described
by the narrator as 'the first place a bomb-designer would visit when he was planning
his plutonium theft. On file there and freely available are the plans of every civilian
nuclear installation in the country.'

The programme seems certain to create enormous controversy – not only over the   25
lack of nuclear safeguards, but also over the morality of commissioning the student to
design a bomb and the wisdom of drawing attention to the ways that a nuclear thief can
work.

Even an official of Public Broadcasting System, which is distributing the TV programme, confessed to qualms: 'It's a terribly important subject, and people should   30

know about the dangers, but I can't help wondering if the programme won't give someone ideas.'

'The Plutonium Connection' explains, for example, that the security systems of
nuclear plants were all designed to prevent sabotage by perhaps one or two agents of
some foreign Power. But now this appears less of a hazard than the possibility of an   35
attack by an armed band of terrorists with dedicated disregard for their own lives.

The programme discusses two major plutonium reprocessing plants in the US – one
already operating in Oklahoma, one being completed in South Carolina – neither of
which has more than a handful of armed guards to supplement the alarms, fences and
gun-detectors that Government security requires. Both are in such remote areas that it   40
would take at least 45 minutes for a sizeable police force to be assembled, if there were an
attack.

An official of the South Carolina plant – a joint operation of Allied Chemical, Gulf
Oil and Royal Dutch Shell – admits to television viewers that the 'system we've designed
would probably not prevent' a band of about 12 armed terrorists from entering.   45

Pilfering plutonium is even easier, the programme suggests. Despite constant inven-
tories, there are inevitably particles of plutonium unaccounted for – about 1 lb a month
at the Oklahoma plant, owned by the Kerr–McGee oil company, which in a year adds
up to enough to make an atomic bomb. It is suggested that pilfering would be even
easier if instrument technicians were unscrupulous enough to alter their measuring   50
devices.

The television film also shows radioactive fuel being transported to nuclear processing
plants in commercial armoured cars. As a safety measure, US drivers of such cars are
ordered to contact headquarters by radio telephone every two hours. But the equipment
is 'cumbersome and unreliable,' and in difficult terrain there are radio blackout areas.   55

The programme ends with a warning from Dr Theodore Taylor, a former Atomic
Energy Commission officer who has long contended that any person of modest technical
ability could make an atomic bomb: 'If we don't get this problem under international
control within the next five or six years, there is a good chance that it will be
permanently out of control.'   60

Report in *The Observer*

1   Why did the student design an atomic bomb?
a) because he was really a terrorist
b) as a normal part of his studies at Massachusetts Institute of Technology
c) as an experiment to see how easy it was
d) as a blackmail weapon

2   Why would a terrorist go to the Atomic Energy Commission's public reading room?
a) to find out how to design a bomb
b) to find out where to steal plutonium
c) to look at files of secret information
d) to find out where to steal an atomic bomb

3   The student found out how to design an atomic bomb
a) from secret information in the Atomic Energy Commission's library.
b) during his course at Massachusetts Institute of Technology.
c) from information made available on television programmes.
d) from information he found in science libraries.

4 The television programme could be criticised because it might
a) teach people how to make bombs.
b) show people how to steal plutonium.
c) put the government in a bad light.
d) give secret information to foreign powers.

5 An official of the organisation distributing the television programme 'confessed to qualms' (line 30). This means
a) he was not sure that the programme should be broadcast.
b) he said that he had behaved dishonestly.
c) he said that even he had thought of stealing plutonium.
d) he explained honestly and openly what he had done.

6 Plutonium plants can easily be robbed because
a) their security precautions do not work properly.
b) they were not planned in such a way as to resist a terrorist attack.
c) a lot of plutonium is stolen.
d) the local police are inefficient.

7 The main danger discussed in the passage is from
a) students making their own atomic bombs.
b) foreign spies stealing secrets.
c) terrorists stealing plutonium and making their own bombs.
d) technicians pilfering plutonium.

8 The sentence 'there's got to be more to it than this' (lines 15–16) means
a) it seems too easy
b) it seems unimportant
c) I should have help from other people
d) I think I should have more equipment

9 In 'It's simple' (line 16), 'it' refers to
a) making an atomic bomb
b) the bomb itself
c) working alone
d) getting the necessary information

10 What does 'this' refer to, in the expression 'this appears less of a hazard' (line 35)?
a) some foreign Power
b) the design of the security systems
c) a terrorist attack
d) sabotage by people working for an enemy country

11 What is 'this problem' (line 58)?
a) how to manufacture atomic bombs
b) how to stamp out terrorism
c) how to stop people stealing plutonium and making their own bombs
d) how to increase security at American nuclear plants

12 What is the main theme of the passage?
a) the fact that a student was able to make an atomic bomb
b) the dangers of transporting plutonium
c) the fact that secret information is available in public libraries
d) the ease with which atomic bombs could become a terrorist weapon

Second passage

Legalising pot

Legalising pot*, as recommended this weekend in a conference resolution of the National Union of Students, is not now as radical a proposal as it might seem. All manner of 'establishment' figures have supported similar plans: from a Presidential Commission in the US to the Principal of King's College, London, who wanted to see the drug taxed and proceeds used for university research. There are, indeed, several unsatisfactory 5
problems created by the present ban on cannabis*: the law is widely disregarded and thus helps to bring other laws into disrespect; it can only be enforced selectively because of the large number of people who use the drug at home: it can lead to unnecessary – and possibly illegal – police searches; and it increases friction between the police and minority groups, like framers of the NUS motion. Finally, if drugs such as cigarettes and alcohol 10
are permitted, then why not pot?

The last point is easy to counter: quasi-Government approval for two harmful drugs is no argument for permitting a third. Unlike drink and tobacco, there is still some doubt about the harmful effects of cannabis, but research here is in its early days. Already Columbia University scientists in New York have completed one project which 15
suggests that the drug could open the door to metabolic diseases, including cancers, by affecting cellular immunity. The team found that white blood cells of cannabis users were 40 per cent less effective in fighting viruses than those of non-cannabis users. Other studies have discovered all manner of side effects, including the danger of growing impotency. Any responsible Government would hold back in such circumstances; not least because 20
the fad appears to be on the wane. To legalise it now might promote the drug just as its use was beginning to decline.

But if Mr Jenkins wants to maintain his reputation as a reformer, there are useful amendments he could make to the law. Far too many people are still ending up in prison – over 700 in 1972 – merely for using the drug. The last Conservative Government 25
finally recognised a sharp distinction which must be made between users and pushers, and cut the maximum sentence for users from twelve months to six. But is prison necessary at all for users, particularly now that criminologists have demonstrated so starkly the damage that prison can cause? In the American state of Oregon, cannabis users are treated like traffic offenders, fined heavily but are never sent to prison. It is 30
right that the big pushers, coining thousands of pounds from their trade, should receive heavy sentences. But the courts must also take note that there are two types of pushers: the professional and the amateur. The latter is often as much a user as a seller in the drug sub-culture. A community service order, which would allow an amateur pusher a chance to contribute to society, seems a far more appropriate sentence than prison. 35

Article in *The Guardian*

1   'Establishment figures' (line 3) means
a) reliable statistics
b) people who work for important organisations
c) people who have power and influence in the country
d) people who have been in their positions for a long time

* *pot*: marihuana (slang)
  cannabis: the same as pot

2 'Helps to bring other laws into disrespect' (line 7) means that
a) drug-takers will break other laws.
b) other laws are needed to control drug-taking.
c) because people can break this law without being caught, other laws are not taken seriously.
d) this law has less value than others.

3 'It can only be enforced selectively' (line 7) means that
a) not all offenders can be punished.
b) it cannot be enforced carefully.
c) only the worst criminals should be arrested.
d) the law does not regard all drugs in the same way.

4 What is the writer's attitude to the argument (in lines 10–11) 'if drugs such as cigarettes and alcohol are permitted, then why not pot?'
a) agreement
b) disagreement
c) uncertainty
d) agreement with reservations

5 What is meant by 'the fad appears to be on the wane' (line 21)?
a) The police are becoming more successful in stamping out drug abuse.
b) There is a change in public attitudes to drug-taking.
c) More people are using pot.
d) Fewer people are using pot.

6 The writer says that according to research that has been carried out, the effects of using pot on health
a) are exaggerated.
b) may be considerable.
c) are not important.
d) are completely unknown.

7 The writer says that 'too many people are ending up in prison . . . merely for using the drug' (lines 24–5). This implies
a) that too many people take cannabis.
b) that people who only use it should not go to prison.
c) that prison sentences are too long.
d) that prison is an unsuitable punishment for all drug offences.

8 The phrase 'coining thousands of pounds from their trade' (line 31) means
a) growing tons of cannabis
b) charging too much for cannabis
c) making false banknotes
d) making fortunes by selling cannabis

9 A 'community service order' (line 34) means
a) a special scheme for reforming drug addicts
b) a way of making convicted drug-sellers contribute to society
c) forcing drug-sellers to do military service
d) a heavy fine instead of prison

10 The writer's main argument is that
a) pot should be legalised.
b) people should be made aware of the moral and medical dangers of drug-taking.

c) the drug laws should be made more humane for all offenders.

d) the laws should be made less severe for people who use pot and for some of those who sell it.

Practice test 9

(Suggested time-limit: 1 hour)
Read the following passage and then answer the questions.

A séance

A good example of this technique of investigating the reliability of reports is an experiment reported by S. J. Davey. He was interested in the kind of phenomena reported during séances* and, using quite simple trickery, which he had planned in advance, he reproduced some of the effects popular among the mediums* of the day. His audiences were asked to write down accounts of what they had witnessed, and these   5
observations were then compared with what actually happened. Here is a report written by one witness of such a séance. 'On entering the dining-room where the séance was held', so the report runs, 'every article of furniture was searched and Mr Davey turned out his pockets. The door was locked and sealed, the gas turned out, and they all sat round the table holding hands, including Mr Davey. A musical box on the table played   10
and floated about. Knockings were heard and bright lights seen. The head of a woman appeared, came close and dematerialized. A half-figure of a man was seen a few seconds later. He bowed and then disappeared through the ceiling with a scraping noise.'

Another witness also described the searching of the room, the sealing of the door, and the disposition of the medium and sitters round the table. She alleged that a female head   15
appeared in a strong light and afterwards a bearded man reading a book, who disappeared through the ceiling. All the while Mr Davey's hands were held tightly by the sitters on either side, and when the gas was relit the door was still locked and the seal unbroken.

A third witness's account was even more sensational. He reported that 'nothing was prepared beforehand, the séance was quite casual'. Having described the locking and   20
sealing of the door, he went on to say that he was touched by a cold, clammy hand and heard various raps. After that he saw a bluish-white light which hovered over the heads of the sitters and gradually developed into an apparition that was 'frightful in its ugliness, but so distinct that everyone could see it... The features were distinct... a kind of hood covered the head, and the whole resembled the head of a mummy'. After this an even   25
more wonderful spirit appeared. It began with a streak of light and developed by degrees into a bearded man of Oriental appearance. His eyes were stony and fixed, with a vacant listless expression. At the end of the séance the door was still locked and the seal was intact.

So much for some of the reports. Now for the reality. The séance was not a casual affair at all, but had been carefully rehearsed beforehand. At the beginning, Mr Davey   30
went through the motion of apparently locking the door, but he turned the key back again so that the door was actually left unlocked. The 'props' for the materializations had been stowed away in a cupboard underneath a bookshelf; this was not looked into by the witnesses who searched the room because, just as they were about to do so, Mr Davey diverted their attention by emptying his pockets to show that he had nothing hidden on   35
his person. The phenomena were produced by a confederate who came in by the un-

* *séances*: attempts to communicate with the dead
  mediums: people who claim to be able to communicate with the dead

locked door after the lights had been turned out, and while the musical box was playing loudly to drown the noise of his entry. The 'apparition of frightful ugliness' was a mask draped in muslin with a cardboard collar coated with luminous paint. The second spirit was the confederate himself, standing on the back of Mr Davey's chair, his face faintly   40
illuminated by phosphorescent light from the pages of a book he was holding. The rasping noise made when the spirits seemed to disappear through the ceiling was caused accidentally, but interpreted by the witnesses according to their conception of what was happening. When the light was turned on the gummed paper that had been used to seal the door had fallen off, but Mr Davey quickly pressed it back into position and then called the witnesses' attention to the fact that it was 'still intact'. Mr Davey's performances   46
were so convincing that some leading investigators, including the biologist A. R. Wallace, F.R.S., refused to believe him when he said that he had no mediumistic powers and it had all been done by trickery. In effect the conjurer was challenged to prove that he was *not* a medium!   50

From *Sense and Nonsense in Psychology* by H. J. Eysenck

1 What was the purpose of S. J. Davey's experiment?
2 Explain the meaning of 'some of the effects popular among the mediums of the day' (line 4).
3 Why was the door locked and sealed?
4 What differences are there between the reports of the first and the second witness?
5 Why were Davey's hands held by his neighbours?
6 Say briefly why the third witness's account was 'even more sensational'.
7 Explain the meaning of the phrase 'carefully rehearsed beforehand' (line 30).
8 What is meant by 'went through the motion of apparently locking the door' (line 31)?
9 What is meant by 'props' (line 32)?
10 Why did the witnesses not find the props?
11 What does the word 'this', in line 33, refer to?
12 'Just as they were about to do so' (line 34). To do what?
13 Why did the witnesses not realise that Mr Davey had an assistant?
14 The word 'it', in line 46, refers to...
15 The word 'it', in line 49, refers to...
16 Explain the difference between a conjuror and a medium, as the words are used in the last sentence of the text.
17 In a paragraph of not more than 100 words, say simply what the witnesses thought happened, and what really happened.

Practice test 10

(Suggested time-limit: 1 hour)
Read the following texts carefully and then answer the questions.

First passage

The biggest flying monster in the world

The largest known creature ever to have flown, an extinct reptile with an estimated wingspan of 51 ft, has been discovered by fossil hunters in west Texas.

The creature, which lived more than 60 million years ago, had twice the wingspan of the biggest previously known pterodactyl, or winged reptile, and nearly six times the wing-span of the condor, the largest bird now alive. 5

The estimated size of the creature is derived from calculations based on the size of many fragmentary, and some complete bones found in excavations during the past three years at Big Bend national park in Brewster County, Texas.

Announcement of the discovery, in the present issue of *Science*, is expected to rekindle an old debate among palaeontologists over whether flying reptiles flapped their 10 featherless, leathery wings or merely climbed on to high perches and leapt into the air currents to soar like gliders.

One scientist familiar with the discovery said that the mammoth size of the newly found creature made improbable the theory that it was able to rise into the air under wing-power alone. He noted, however, that the lack of a reliable estimate of the 15 reptile's weight virtually precluded any calculation of its aerodynamic properties.

The fossils were found by Mr Douglas Lawson, a graduate student at the University of California, who began searching in the Big Bend area while a student at Texas University. His continuing explorations and study of the fossils are being carried out under the auspices of the university's vertebrate palaeontology laboratory. 20

Although the reptile clearly represents a new species, it has not yet been given a formal scientific name. There are many known species of flying reptiles. Scientists generally refer to all as pterosaurs, but the popular name pterodactyl is also considered correct. All are extinct.

'What's so extraordinary about this thing is its tremendous size', Dr Wann Langston, 25 director of the vertebrate palaeontology laboratory, said. 'There has never been any-thing like this before.'

In his report Mr Lawson says he has discovered the partial skeletons of three of the large pterosaurs, including the remains of four wings, a neck, the hind legs (forelimbs with claws are frequently part of the wing structure), and jaws, which were toothless. 30

Unlike most previously known pterosaurs, the Big Bend creature was found in non-marine sediments, suggesting that its habitat was away from oceans. Most pterosaurs are considered to have been fish eaters, scooping up their prey while gliding over the waves.

The Big Bend fossils were found in fresh-water sediments far from the oceans of that 35 time. In his report Mr Lawson writes that the reptile's unusually long neck suggests it may have been a carrion-eater, feeding on dead dinosaurs, much as the condors and other vultures of today consume dead animals.

Second passage

Monster could not flap wings

The extinct reptile with an estimated wingspan of 51 ft, found by fossil hunters in western Texas, would have been a warm-blooded creature, with a furry coat like that of a 40 mammal, according to Mr Adrian Desmond, of Harvard University museum of com-parative zoology.

Mr Desmond, who is in England writing a book about dinosaurs and pterosaurs, said yesterday that the creature was much larger than any pterosaur – the popular name of which is pterodactyl – found before. The one found in 1970 in Soviet Kazakhstan was 45 furry.

'It is wrong to think that the pterodactyl had featherless, leathery wings, because

they were warm-blooded creatures, and the one found in Russia had furry wings, and
fur on its fingers', he said. 'In that, they were like mammals, although they are called
reptiles.'   50

The size of the creature found in the Big Bend national park in Brewster County,
Texas, was derived from calculations based on the size of many fragmentary, and
some complete bones, excavated over the past three years.

Mr Desmond said that it would not have flapped its wings, because they would be
too heavy for the creature to cope with if flapped. It would simply have raised them   55
and floated into the air when it wished to fly.

'The find is much larger than anything discovered before. The largest one found
before the Texas excavation had a wingspan of 23 ft, and the latest find is extraordinary
because it was never thought that there could be anything bigger. It is very fascinating
indeed.'   60

Reports from *The Times*

1 What is especially interesting about the discovery described in the texts?
2 How do scientists manage to have an idea of how big the creature was?
3 Rewrite the expression 'to rekindle an old debate' (lines 9–10) in other words (you
   may repeat the word 'old' if you wish).
4 Why did the scientist quoted in the fifth paragraph of the first text think it unlikely
   that the creature could have taken off from the ground?
5 Rewrite in more simple language 'the lack of a reliable estimate of the reptile's weight
   virtually precluded any calculation of its aerodynamic properties' (lines 15–16).
6 What does the word 'all' refer to, in line 23?
7 The researchers have not found the remains of any front legs. What explanation for
   this is suggested in the first passage?
8 What appears to have been the difference between this creature's way of life and that
   of other flying reptiles?
9 What is the evidence for the belief that the creature did not live near the sea?
10 What does the word 'that' refer to, in line 40?
11 What suggestion in the first article is contradicted by the second?
12 What is meant by the word 'that', in line 49?
13 The word 'one', in line 57, refers to...
14 Say exactly what is meant by the expression 'anything bigger', in line 59.
15 What does the second 'it', in line 59, refer to?
16 In a paragraph of not more than 100 words, sum up the discovery described in the
   two articles, saying what is known and what is still not known about the creature.

Practice test 11

(Suggested time-limit: 1 hour)
Read the following passage and then answer the questions.

Grammar school

The first weeks at grammar school were strange. For the children who already had
contacts, they were exhilarating, the exciting prelude to promised satisfactions. Whole
new areas of inviting study presented themselves – algebra, physics, Latin, French.

'I took to Marburton College like a duck to water,' said Ronald Turnbull. For children who had broken most friendships and connexions with the old neighbourhood, here were fresh children, fresh clubs and societies, the school scouts and the school corps to join. The invitation was irresistible, and many were glad to accept it in full and become from the earliest days loyal and eager members of the school. Their whole-heartedness was naturally reflected in their first pieces of work, and finding themselves soon well placed in class, they were conscious of latent power thrusting through, of their ability to command new and more testing situations. We have shown that most of the parents came from the very upper reaches of the working-class, and once their child reached grammar school, these parents were whole-heartedly behind the enterprise. In very many small ways they influenced their children to accept, to belong. Both grammar school and home supported the child in orthodox and receptive attitudes. But under particular strains and pressures, this home support could, and did, break down; and this happens more and more often as either the school disturbs the parents (directly in an interview, indirectly through weight of homework and so on), or the parents find no way of obtaining vital knowledge, or coming to terms with the middle-class ethos of the grammar school. The parents may have been 'sunken middle-class', but many of these discover how different this can be in knowledge and evaluation from that range of middle-class life endorsed by the grammar school.

For the majority of the children, unlike Ronald Turnbull, the entry to grammar school was uncertain and confused. They had suddenly lost in some measure that mesh of securities, expectations, recognitions, that we have called 'neighbourhood'. 'I had this feeling of not *belonging* anywhere,' said Patricia Joy. They found themselves surrounded by more middle-class children than they had ever met before. These children spoke better, seemed more confident, some already knew bits of French and Latin, their fathers had told them what 'Physics' was about, a few even knew the teachers. *They*, evidently, seemed to belong. This insecurity was heightened by confusions over getting the right books, the right sports equipment, the right uniform. 'I didn't like it,' said Rita Watson, 'my uniform seemed too big all round – long sleeves – I suppose my mother had to do it like that so it would last longer, but I felt awful. All the other girls' uniforms seemed all right. *I* was wrong.' On top of this came the new subjects, the new vocabulary (not 'kept in' but 'detention', not 'playtime' but 'break' – and was it 'yard' or 'playground' or 'cloisters'?), the masters' gowns, the prefects, the whole body of customs, small rights and wrongs, that any well-developed grammar school holds. Some of the schools made a practice of teaching the new children aggressively for the first weeks, to 'break them in', and, presumably, to nip behaviour problems in the bud. The effect on children already bewildered was to knock them off balance rather than 'break them in' and to create, rather than cure, behaviour problems. This was obvious in our study of the middle-class child where a highly gifted boy could be so robbed of confidence in the first term, as to *seem* dull for several years afterwards. For some of the working-class children, confused by a genuine loss of part of their social life ('Neighbourhood'), perplexed by the strangeness and sheer difference of grammar school, conscious of new *social* barriers thickening the normal barriers between pupil and teacher, and unable to turn to parents for explanation and understanding – for these children the beginnings could seem almost hallucinatory. 'I had that feeling like when you were in the forces,' said one boy, 'after you got your jabs and you got inoculation fever, you felt away from it all. You felt in a bit of a haze, everything was a bit bleared. Well, that's how school felt at first. I felt just as I did later when I'd got inoculation fever.'

From *Education and the Working Class* by Brian Jackson and Dennis Marsden

1 What is meant by 'children who already had contacts' (lines 1–2)?
2 'They', in line 2, refers to...
3 Explain 'I took to Marburton College like a duck to water' (line 4).
4 What is meant by 'the old neighbourhood' (line 5)?
5 Write in another way 'Their wholeheartedness was naturally reflected in their first pieces of work' (lines 8–9).
6 What is meant by the expression 'testing situations' (line 11)?
7 '...they influenced their children to accept, to belong' (line 14). To accept what and to belong to what?
8 What sort of class background did most of the grammar school children come from, according to the passage?
9 What does the second 'this', in line 16, refer to?
10 Why did Patricia Joy have a feeling of 'not belonging' (line 26)?
11 Who are 'they' in line 26?
12 Who are 'these children' in line 27?
13 What does 'it', in line 31, refer to?
14 'To break them in' (lines 38–9) means...
15 'This', in line 41, means...
16 Why were the children referred to in lines 39–40 'already bewildered'?
17 Some children were 'unable to turn to parents for explanation and understanding' (lines 46–7) because...
18 Write a paragraph of not more than 100 words summing up the problems which, according to the author, faced working-class children when they went to grammar school.

Practice test 12

(Suggested time-limit: 1 hour)
Read the following text and then answer the questions.

Gunfight in Pickering City

Meanwhile, back at the livery stable, four men with eyes like a cheap wholesale grade of domestic caramels stepped out into the main street. In forbidding silence they arrayed themselves from sidewalk to sidewalk across that street, evenly spaced with Moses and Segal flanking Roth and Ragaway in the middle. They began their grim walk. It was a stiff wooden-legged lurch which was to be imitated by so many gunfighters throughout the West as the years went on.   5

Abe Weiler, the only doctor in Pickering City and publisher-editor of Pickering City's only newspaper, the crusading *Times*, a monthly, saw them coming. Made spry by the danger and the circulation-stimulating story it presaged, to say nothing of the active medical opportunities which could follow, he rushed across the street and into the   10
dry-goods store dead ahead.

Evaliña stood in front of the two young men and pleaded with them, trying to make them focus on their peril, trying to make them focus on anything. 'Jim! Irish!' she said. 'Ragaway and Roth are coming to gun you down. *Irish! Jim!* Ragaway and Roth are coming!'   15

'Honey, I tell you you are an absolutely gorgeous thing,' Irish said. Street bobbed his head up and down.

In despair she ran to the front window of the saloon and peered through the curtains at the direction of the livery stable. She saw the four men. She saw the eight guns on their hips. She saw the forty-eight pieces of lead but did not actually compute that far as they had not yet come to multiplication at the Academy. She knew only one way to stop them.

Street stumbled to his feet. He stared down at Irish.

'Roth'n Ragaway,' he said, 'lookin' for sawdust in their beards.'

'*Sí*.'

'Putcher boots on.'

'*Sí*.' Irish bent over but kept going down. He sat on the floor and put one boot on. He could not find the other boot. He looked up at his partner helplessly.

'Who neez boots,' Street interrogated.

'*Sí*'.

Irish pulled himself to his feet by clinging to Jim's pants. He was a heavy man desperate to right himself. The trousers ripped, but only in the back. Irish made it to his feet, but Street's whole rear section flapped as he turned.

'Whereza gunz?' Jim asked rhetorically. They scanned the room several times. Irish spotted Franklin Heller's gun belt hanging on a hook at the end of the bar. He started towards it, walking as though his right foot were in a shallow trench and his left foot on a minor shelf because he was unaccustomed to walking with only one two-inch heel.

Franklin Heller had never worn this gun belt because the outfit in East New York who had shipped it to him had mistakenly sent him one which was many sizes too large, and Heller had a sixty-one-inch waistline to begin with. Irish took the belt off the hook and slung it around behind him reflexively. Street was standing directly behind his friend. He caught the end of the belt and passed it around in front of them. They buckled it. With cold eyes and a lot of death on each hip, their inside arms bound closely to their sides between them, they moved with the lithe grace of cowhands towards the door and what waited for them in the street outside, Irish limping somewhat badly due to the imbalance caused by wearing just one boot, and Jim chancing lumbago or worse due to the exposure of his lower rear section.

'Something's wrong here,' Irish mumbled as they reached the door.

'We forgot our hats,' Jim explained. 'But the hell with that.' Somehow they made it out to the centre of the street.

Evaliña had found Irish's six-gun. She moved along, close to the building line towards the livery stable, her eyes never leaving the slow advance of the four gunmen. When she was directly across the street from the bank where her father was luxuriating in an all-night poker session with the bank president, the sheriff, and Frank Braden, the advance man for a stunt balloonist, she turned to investigate the sounds of Reyes and Street, bound together like Ishmael and Queequeg with one belt, two guns, three boots, and no hats between them as they staggered into the deserted street, their faces set in the iron mold of men who play to win.

She fired a snap-shot through the bank window. There was a shatter of glass and a shout of horror. The advancing line of gunmen halted uncertainly. Reyes and Street went for their guns, to learn confusedly that their inside arms were strapped in. Major Patten came vaulting out of the broken window, a gun in each hand. 'Who shot the sheriff?' he yelled.

'*Pal*' Evaliña cried out, diverting the disconcerted cow thieves for an instant more. 'It's Roth and Ragaway! They aim to kill our boys!'

Irish fired. Evaliña fired. Jim fired. But each shot followed four shots in dazzling rapid succession from the two guns of Major Patten. Four dead cow thieves were stretched out on the main street of Pickering City.

'They reached and they fumbled an' it was a fatal weakness,' reported the major, holstering his guns. 'Roth and Ragaway was a bad element.'

'Oh Pa!' Evaliña wailed. 'Did Sheriff Kullers lean on my bullet goin' past?'

'Never mind, hon,' her father said proudly. 'Yuh done real good. You'll do to ride the river with.'

70

From *A Talent for Loving* by Richard Condon

1 Why was Abe Weiler pleased at the prospect of a gunfight?
2 How many different men do the names Jim, Irish, Street and Reyes refer to?
3 Why did the two young men find it difficult to 'focus on anything' (line 13)?
4 Where was Evaliña at the beginning of the episode?
5 What is meant by 'they had not yet come to multiplication at the Academy' (lines 20–1)?
6 'She knew only one way to stop them' (lines 21–2). What was this?
7 Explain the expression 'lookin' for sawdust in their beards' (line 24).
8 Why does Street say 'Putcher boots on' instead of 'Put your boots on' and 'Who neez boots' instead of 'Who needs boots' (lines 26 and 29)?
9 'It', in line 36, refers to...
10 Why did Irish have difficulty in walking?
11 Explain the expression 'a lot of death on each hip' (line 43).
12 Their inside arms were 'bound closely to their sides' (lines 43–4) because...
13 What did Jim mean by 'the hell with that' (line 49)?
14 Why did Evaliña fire through the bank window?
15 What was the reason for the 'shout of horror' (line 60)?
16 Why were the cow thieves slow to draw their guns?
17 Who shot the sheriff?
18 Sum up clearly the events described in the passage, in a paragraph of not more than 100 words.